Betta and Gouramis

Fish Keeping

Made Easy™

Bettas and Gouramis

Understanding Siamese Fighting Fish,
Paradisefish, Kissing Gouramis, and
Other Anabantoids

David Alderton

BOWTIE™
P R E S S

Irvine, California

Published in 2004 by BowTie Press
A Division of Fancy Publications
3 Burroughs, Irvine, CA 92618
www.bowtiepress.com
Fish Keeping Made Easy is an imprint of BowTie Press

Produced by Andromeda Oxford Limited
Kimber House
1 Kimber Road
Abingdon
Oxon OX14 1SG.
www.andromeda.co.uk

Project Director: Graham Bateman. Managing Editor: Shaun Barrington.
Editing and design: D & N DTP and Editorial Services.
Cartography: Tim Williams. Indexer: Sheila Seacroft.
Picture Manager: Claire Turner. Production: Clive Sparling.

Library of Congress Cataloging-in-Publication Data
Alderton, David, 1956-
  Bettas and gouramis / by David Alderton.-- 1st ed.
     p. cm. -- (Fishkeeping made easy)
  ISBN 1-931993-13-0 (hardcover : alk. paper)
  1. Betta. 2. Gourami. I. Title. II. Series.

SF458.B4A43 2003
639.3'77--dc21

                              2003012794

Page 2: Golden gourami (*Trichogaster trichopterus* var.).
Cover: Siamese fighting fish (*Betta splendens* var.); Max Gibbs/Photomax.

Photographic credits: H = www.Hippocampus-Bildarchiv.de
Andromeda Oxford Limited 67 x3; David Armitage 120c, 120b; Matthew Wright/Been There Done That 68, 108; ACS/Frank Teigler/H 3, 28, 31l, 36, 42, 115, 124c, 134, 136; Dieter Bork/H 20, 27, 35; Frank Shäfer/H 15, 22, 38, 49, 71, 91t, 91ctl, 91ctr, 91cbl, 91cbr, 91bl, 91br, 94, 118; G. Schreiber/H 53; © www.Hippocampus-Bildarchiv.de 3, 7, 10, 16–17, 23, 25, 26, 30, 31r, 33, 37, 40, 43, 45, 47, 48, 50, 51, 52, 54, 57, 58, 76, 88, 90tl, 90tr, 90cl, 90cr, 90bl, 93, 97, 99, 110, 114c, 114b, 116, 119, 121, 122c, 123, 124b, 125, 126, 127, 128, 130c, 130b, 131, 132, 133, 135, 137; Max Gibbs/Photomax 2, 6, 13b, 14, 16, 18–19, 24, 39, 56, 61, 63, 64, 65, 66, 72, 72–73, 75, 77, 81, 100, 101, 106, 109, 112, 113, 117, 122b, 129; Mike Sandford 13c, 44, 59, 78, 79, 83, 85, 86, 87; Jane Burton/Warren Photographic 12, 62, 74, 82, 92, 96, 102

Color origination by Grasmere Digital Imaging Ltd., Leeds.
Printed in Hong Kong by Paramount Printing Ltd.

Contents

Nature and Nurture

When bettas and gouramis were first kept is unknown. What is certain is that these fish were popular in their Asiatic homeland for centuries before they became known in the West. Paradisefish (Macropodus opercularis), the hardiest member of the group, may have been seen in London during the mid-1600s, with fish corresponding to their description being recorded there by the famous diarist Samuel Pepys.

There is a considerable range in size in the anabantoids, as these fish are collectively known, from the tiny licorice gourami (*Parosphromenus parvulus*), measuring barely 1.5in (4cm), up to the giant gourami (*Osphronemus goramy*), which can grow to 28in (70cm) and may weigh more than 15lb (7kg). The ease with which these large fish can be bred and reared, under what would normally be considered fairly poor environmental conditions, led to the start of the fish farming industry in Asia.

⬇ Paradisefish (*Macropodus opercularis*) are among the most easily kept bettas, and make an excellent introduction to this group of fish.

Initial human interest in anabantoids was therefore as food. This was especially significant in a tropical region of the world, well before the development of refrigeration. Fresh fish would spoil readily in the heat, but an essential component of the biology of this group meant that this factor was less significant in their case, making them an attractive proposition to rear commercially. In

contrast to most other fish, anabantoids are able to breathe air directly, thanks to their labyrinth organs. As a result, they could be transported alive out of water, arriving in a relatively fresh state at their destination.

Fish keeping for pleasure also features prominently within Asiatic culture, as shown by the domestication of other species such as goldfish and koi in this part of the world. Smaller labyrinth fish have been bred there in a wide range of fancy forms, notably the Siamese fighting fish (*Betta splendens*).

It was soon obvious that it was not only their appearance that could be modified, leading to the development of much more elaborate fins, but also their temperament. Their level of aggression could be increased through selective breeding. This led to the creation of fighting competitions, a tradition that continues to the present day in Thailand, with large amounts being wagered on contests between individual fish. This particular betta remains the most widely kept anabantoid today, both in its homeland and also in the U.S., where it consistently ranks in the most popular ten species out of all tropical aquarium fish.

With hundreds of years of selective breeding having taken place, it is now impossible to unravel the original distribution or even the appearance of the ancestral form of these fish. The first Siamese fighting fish reached Europe alive in 1894 and were bred by their French importer soon afterward. Since those early days, a huge commercial breeding operation has developed in Southeast Asia, in centers such as Singapore, where these and other anabantoids are raised in massive numbers for the aquarium trade worldwide. There is also a significant commercial farming of members of these ornamental fish in Florida, where the U.S. aquarium fish industry grew up after the end of World War II in the late 1940s.

⬆ Many bettas and gouramis are found in the wild in shallow stretches of water, such as this stream in southern Thailand. Throughout this book, insights into natural fish behavior are emphasized. Understanding how a fish lives in the wild leads to a better understanding of how it should be looked after in the aquarium.

CHAPTER 1

Where in the World?

The natural distribution of labyrinth fish today extends eastward right across India and Southeast Asia to the Moluccan Islands of Indonesia as well as the Philippines and Taiwan. Members of the group range northward into northern China, beyond Korea. A totally separate population of African labyrinth fish occurs south of the Sahara, although they are absent from much of eastern Africa as well as Madagascar.

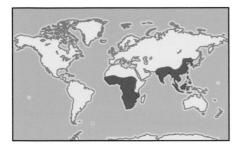

⬆ The natural distribution of anabantoids is restricted to parts of Southeast Asia and Africa.

This division in the distribution of members of the anabantoid family is explained by the way in which the continents have divided in the Earth's past. These geological shifts occurring over the course of millions of years help to explain the distribution of the labyrinth fish today.

Unfortunately, relatively little is known from the fossil record about the ancestry of today's anabantoids. They were almost certainly represented on the eastern side of the massive formative southern continent known as Gondwanaland, probably at a stage after what was to become South America separated off from what is now the western side of present-day Africa. This helps to explain why there are no representatives of the anabantoid group found naturally in the Americas today.

What has since become the Indian subcontinent formed part of the northeastern region of Gondwanaland, and this split off too, slowly drifting northward until it collided with the rest of Asia, carrying the ancestors of today's Asiatic anabantoids northward. Here they developed in isolation and have tended to become more specialized in their habits than their African relatives.

A CHANGING LANDSCAPE

In common with other vertebrates, the easterly range of this group of fish in Asia was restricted, extending as far as what has now become known as Wallace's Line. This biological phenomenon was first observed by the zoologist Alfred Russel Wallace, who was a contemporary of Charles Darwin and is credited with inspiring his theory of evolution. He noted how the bird life altered dramatically between the island of Bali and that of Lombok, lying some 20 miles (32km) to the east. The channel between these islands has

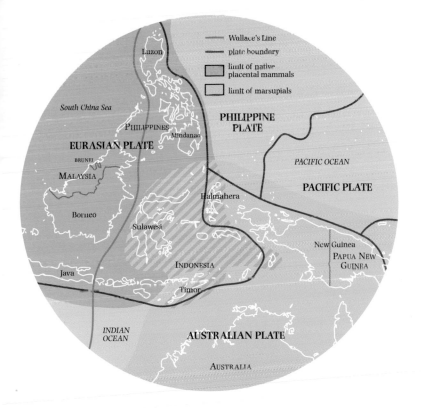

	Wallace's Line
	plate boundary
	limit of native placental mammals
	limit of marsupials

Luzon

South China Sea

PHILIPPINES
Mindanao

PHILIPPINE PLATE

EURASIAN PLATE

BRUNEI

MALAYSIA

PACIFIC OCEAN

PACIFIC PLATE

Halmahera

Borneo

Sulawesi

New Guinea
PAPUA NEW GUINEA

Java

INDONESIA

Timor

INDIAN OCEAN

AUSTRALIAN PLATE

AUSTRALIA

come to mark the division between the range of Oriental and Australian species. Wallace observed a continuation of this phenomenon farther north, between the islands of Borneo and Sulawesi (formerly Celebes), and sought to explain this apparent barrier to the movement of species on the basis of geological changes that had occurred quite recently through the region.

During the Ice Ages the sea level fell, as more of the world's water was trapped as ice. Areas to the west of Wallace's line were then attached to the Asian mainland, with interconnecting rivers between what are now isolated islands such as Sumatra and Borneo enabling fish such as gouramis to move between these localities, without having to enter the marine environment.

In *Trichogaster* gouramis, this explains why the spotted gourami (*T. trichopterus*) can be found today not only in Southeast Asia, but also on both of these islands. During interglacial periods, as the ice caps melted, there was a corresponding rise in sea level. This resulted in flooding of the lower lying areas of the world and was responsible for the creation of the islands that exist in the region today.

🔾 Changing sea levels in the past have had a marked effect on the range of anabantoids today, specifically in Southeast Asia. The easterly limit of their range falls on Wallace's Line, where species of Oriental and Australian origins meet.

● Distinctive races of gouramis that have evolved as individual populations have been isolated by environmental changes. The blue gourami (*Trichogaster trichogaster sumatranus*) shown here is one of the best-known examples of this phenomenon in the aquarium hobby.

As a result, these populations of anabantoids were cut off from each other, becoming separated by the surrounding sea. Subsequent selection pressure caused by further isolation in some parts of its range, notably in western Sumatra, has led to the creation of the distinctive blue subspecies, *T.t. sumatranus*, of the spotted gourami.

Wallace's Line also suggests that where there are populations of *Trichogaster* and indeed other gouramis to the east of this zoogeographic border, on some of the Lesser Sunda islands such as Sumbawa, the likelihood is that these were introduced there by the human population. There is a long tradition of various Asiatic anabantoids being moved to new habitats, because of their value as food.

DIFFERENT WAYS OF BREATHING AIR

The first bony fish evolved some 410 million years ago, but it was not until recently, in evolutionary terms, that the labyrinth fish gained the feature that helps to distinguish it today. Fossil evidence suggests that it was around 60 million years ago, just after the dinosaur era, that the first indications of this feature became apparent in their ancestral lineage.

Yet the anabantoids were not the first fish to be able to breathe air, rather than having to rely on their gills to extract oxygen from the water. The Lungfish (dipnoans) for example have a long history in the fossil record, dating back almost as far as the development of bony fish themselves. They originally inhabited the sea, but by about 340 million years ago, they had adapted entirely to freshwater. There are three surviving groups of lungfish in the world today, which are found respectively in parts of South America, Africa, and Australia, where the most primitive form occurs.

Lungfish used to be much more widely distributed, as revealed by their fossilized remains, which have been uncovered as far apart as China and Scotland. The lungs of these fish actually represent a modification of the air sacs, which were present in the earliest bony fish. These structures were connected directly with the gut, and provided buoyancy for the fish.

These air sacs assumed a respiratory function in the lungfish. This was achieved simply by folding, which increased their surface

area, combined with increasing vascularization to improve the exchange of oxygen and carbon dioxide, thanks to the more efficient blood supply. In the ray-finned fish, known as teleosts, which include anabantoids, the air sacs have been replaced by the so-called swim bladder, which sits above and behind the throat. It may still retain a connection here, although generally, as in the anabantoids, it forms a separate structure, through which some gaseous exchange can occur.

The modifications seen in lungfish provide an efficient alternative respiratory system, extracting oxygen directly from the air, rather than from water flowing over the gills. The importance of this mechanism is still evident if these fish become trapped.

❶ Air-breathing is not a recent occurrence in fish, nor is it confined solely to anabantoids. Lungfish are one of the other groups that can meet their oxygen requirement in part by this means.

Being able to breathe air ensures that lungfish can estivate, (pass the summer or dry season in a dormant condition), by burying themselves in the mud as water evaporates from a drying pool. Here, cocooned out of sight, with their metabolic rate slowed and their oxygen requirement minimized, lungfish are capable of surviving for months until the rains come again, replenishing the water in their pools and allowing them to continue their aquatic existence.

The evolutionary pressure for this anatomical development may have been induced by climate change during the Devonian period, some 400 million years ago, with the fossil record revealing the dramatic anatomical alterations that occurred in this group of fish at that time. Since then, their lifestyles have not altered significantly, through to today.

⊕ Many anabantoids use air in the form of bubbles to create nests for their eggs, as well as being able to breathe directly at the surface.

The ability to breathe air directly brings distinctive survival benefits when faced with deteriorating environmental conditions. In Africa, while lungfish estivate, others like the annual killifish, in the genus *Aphyosemion*, gear their breeding cycle to this change, spawning just as the pools in which they live dry up. While the adult fish die, the next generation survives as eggs encased in the

mud. Here they remain, waiting for the rains to come, at which point they hatch out.

Labyrinth fish are able to adopt a more active individual survival response in some cases, with the aptly named African bushfish (*Ctenopoma* sp.) being able to drag itself overland using spines on its gills like limbs, in search of other areas of water when its existing habitat dries up.

THE EARLIEST ANABANTOID?

Although there is some dispute among ichthyologists about the ancestral form of the labyrinth fish, it has been suggested that the chameleon fish (*Badis badis*) found in India may provide a link with their past, in spite of the fact that it does not have labyrinth organs. Its common name stems from its ability to change color easily to blend in with the surroundings.

Fish not currently classified as anabantoids also possess labyrinth organs. Snakeheads form the family Channidae, grouped in the order Channiformes and, although the temptation to categorize them with anabantoids is obvious on the basis of this unusual anatomical feature, current thinking is that these families represent different evolutionary lines. Both have simply responded to the environmental pressures resulting from their habitat by developing a similar auxiliary method of breathing, which enables them to live in poorly oxygenated and shallow water.

If there was any doubt about the effect that lifestyles can have in shaping the anatomical features of unrelated fish, a clear example can be seen in the pikeheads (*Luciocephalus* spp.), which belong to the anabantoid group. Their physical profile is similar to that of the completely unrelated and much larger pike (*Esox lucius*). Both have a similar predatory nature, with a combination of their habitats and lifestyle molding their appearance on similar lines. Their streamlining and power makes them highly effective ambush predators. This phenomenon, when there is environmental pressure rather than a genetic relationship responsible for shaping similar physical characteristics, is known as convergent evolution.

⊕ The similarity in appearance between the predatory anabantoid known as the pikehead (*Luciocephalus pulcher*) and the much larger, unrelated pike (*Esox lucius*) shown below is a direct reflection of the similarity in their lifestyles.

It is no coincidence that snakeheads have a similar auxiliary breathing system to that of anabantoids, since they inhabit similar environments in both Africa and Asia. In this instance, though, there has been no convergence in their physical appearance, with the body shape and also the size of snakeheads and anabantoids differing significantly. Snakeheads generally have a more elongated body shape. The Indian snakehead (*Channa marulia*) can grow as large as 4ft (1.2m), with the majority of species being significantly bigger even than most gouramis.

The breeding habits of snakeheads are suggestive of those of some anabantoids, in that their eggs float and are guarded by the male, although there is no attempt to construct a nest of any type for them. Again, however, this may be linked to the habitat in which they occur, rather than being suggestive of a close relationship between these fish.

◑ The chameleon fish (*Badis badis*) is classified in the family Nandidae, a group of fish thought by some authorities to have some affinity with the anabantoids, but this is not unversally accepted.

NEW WORLD LINKS

Similarly in South America, there are some fish that are regarded as being allied to anabantoids, on the basis of their physical characteristics, but are not closely related to the group. The family Nandidae, which includes the chameleon fish (*Badis badis*), also features the South American leaf fish in a separate subfamily,

Nandinae. This species does not possess a labyrinth organ, and parental care where practiced consists solely of the male guarding eggs that are deposited on a leaf or similar site, rather than being incorporated into a special nest.

WHY HAVE LABYRINTH ORGANS?

The extent to which anabantoids rely on their labyrinth organs to assist their respiration varies markedly among species. In some cases, these structures appear to have relatively little significance. The need for auxiliary air-breathing is a reflection of the waters in which the majority of species occur. These are typically shallow, slow-flowing, and usually heavily overgrown with algae.

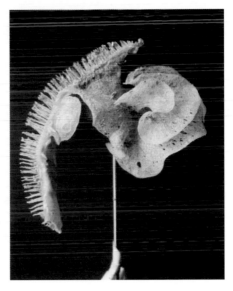

The heat of the tropical sun beating down on shallow stretches of water has the immediate impact of raising the temperature significantly. Many anabantoids occur in waters where the temperature routinely rises to 90° Fahrenheit (32° Celsius) or above during the heat of day. This may even cause them to retreat when possible, out of flooded rice paddies into deeper and thus cooler surrounding stretches of water. There are corresponding chemical changes associated with this rise in water temperature. The most significant is that the amount of oxygen present in solution declines, so there will be less passing over the fishes' gills. The rising water temperature may increase the level of activity of the anabantoids, and thus their oxygen requirement.

Furthermore, the warmth and sunlight together combine to stimulate the growth of aquatic plants, including microscopic algae that may carpet much of the surface, making swimming difficult. At night, these plants take oxygen from the water, when they are not photosynthesizing, while during the daytime, thanks to the water temperature, much of the oxygen they produce is lost, diffusing directly out of the still water in streams of bubbles.

It is possible to predict the environment in which different species of labyrinth fish occur based on the structure of the labyrinth organs. Where environmental conditions are poor, not only are the labyrinth organs larger, but they also have an increased surface area, to facilitate the absorption of atmospheric oxygen.

🔴 The labyrinth organ has a large surface area, so that oxygen can diffuse efficiently into the blood stream, with carbon dioxide exiting from the body by the same route in the pharyngeal region of the throat. Note its close proximity to the gill on the left, doing the same job.

Members of the two African genera of labyrinth fish, *Ctenopoma* and *Sandelia*, found in relatively clear stretches of water, including rivers, have less developed labyrinth organs than the vast majority of their Asiatic relatives. In the predatory pikehead (*Luciocephalus* species), it is thought that these organs may be more significant in detecting and amplifying sounds in the water, rather than being used primarily for respiratory purposes.

OBTAINING OXYGEN

There are other groups of fish that have also evolved supplementary means of breathing under conditions where the oxygen level in the water is low. Notable among these are various species of catfish. This is most apparent in the *Corydoras* species. They lack scales on their bodies, being protected instead by bony plates. These may cause an increased oxygen requirement, which cannot be met from respiration through the gills alone.

As a consequence, they will breathe air directly on a regular basis, darting up to the water's surface for this purpose. Similar behavior is also displayed by the related *Callichthys* genus, and appears to be critical to their survival.

There are catfish that can move on land just like the climbing perch (*Anabas testudineus*) and members of the genus *Ctenopoma*, in search of new stretches of water when environmental conditions deteriorate. They have evolved a different means of meeting their oxygen needs out of water, but it is not entirely dissimilar to that of anabantoids. The gill cavities are enlarged and have highly vascularized areas which enable gaseous exchange to take place, using atmospheric oxygen.

◐ Corvdoras (*Corydoras* sp.) catfish are another group that are able to breathe atmospheric oxygen, but in this case, they simply gulp down air from the surface into their gut.

WHAT'S IN A NAME?

The Asiatic gouramis are broadly divided into two groups—the bettas and the gouramis. The collective description of "betta" that is used for many of the smaller species, including the Siamese fighting fish (*Betta splendens*) itself, is derived from their scientific name. The term "gourami," which is the common name for a number of Asiatic genera, stems from the specific name given to the giant gourami, *Osphronemus goramy*. In this case, the spelling has changed at some time.

Once the scientific name of a species has been published, it is not possible to correct any spelling errors, although this does not apply to common names. This is why sometimes these fish are described as the giant goramy, and by others as the giant gourami, which tends to be the favored option today.

◑ The ability to breathe out of the water has enabled some anabantoids, such as the climbing perch (*Anabas testudineus*), to move over land in search of new habitats.

CHAPTER 2

The Different Groups

The popularity of anabantoids means that a good choice of the most widely kept species can be found at virtually all aquatic stores. There are over 100 anabantoids currently available in the hobby. Many are color varieties of the same species . Bear in mind that you are most likely to be offered young fish, which will be much smaller and frequently less territorial by nature than adults.

Color varieties have been developed in certain groups, especially among *Trichogaster* gouramis, but the widest selection exists in the Siamese fighting fish (*Betta splendens*), where the structure of the fins has also been modified as a result of selective breeding. If you are seeking a particular variant in this case, you may have to find a specialist breeder.

There are a number of societies and also various Web sites catering to those with a particular interest in these fish, so it is not difficult to locate such breeders, especially sincw they often advertise in the columns of the fish keeping magazines. Although it is preferable to visit and choose your own fish it is possible to have fish sent to you safely, particularly if the vendor ships regularly to customers in other parts of the country.

Bear in mind the prevailing weather conditions, and if the temperature is low, it will be better to wait until it rises again. Although the fish may appear unaffected, stressful shipping conditions increase the likelihood of them falling ill soon after their arrival. This is especially significant with some anabantoids, such as the wine red fighter (*Betta coccina*), which is susceptible to velvet disease, caused by the microscopic oodinium parasite. A low temperature lessens the fish's ability to fight infection, allowing these parasites to overwhelm its immune system, resulting in illness (*see* page 105).

MAKING CHOICES

Choosing healthy fish in the first instance is vital. When purchasing anabantoids, be sure to start by looking at all the fish in the tank, rather than focusing immediately on those that catch your eye. This is because if there are any obviously sick fish here, the likelihood is that the infection is present in the water, so the other tank occupants are equally at risk of falling ill, even if they are not showing symptoms at this stage.

Gouramis tend to occupy the upper part of the aquarium, so it is not a matter of concern that the fish congregate here rather than swimming around close to the floor of the tank. Nor are they particularly strong swimmers, but any that hang at an abnormal angle in the water are likely to be sick.

The condition of the fins is important, partly because these enable pairs to be distinguished reliably in a number of cases. Any damage to these areas of the body may make sexing difficult, since it is often the longer projections on the dorsal and anal fins, characteristic of male fish that are affected. These areas can easily become infected. Unless rapid action is taken, the fish's condition is likely to deteriorate. Minor fin damage can heal over the course of several weeks, provided that the fish's environmental conditions are improved, so this is not necessarily a bar to buying an individual that may not be in top condition. However, if there are obvious signs of infection, such as a fungal halo at the site of the injury, then the risk is significantly greater.

⬇ When planning to keep anabantoids, remember that some species will grow to a large size and of course require more space. This aquarium contains the opaline variety of the spotted gourami (*Trichogaster trichopterus*), which can grow to 6in (16cm), but usually does not attain that size in the aquarium.

The age of most anabantoids offered for sale will be unknown if they are fully grown, unless you are buying from a breeder, or perhaps a dealer who sources stock locally. There is unfortunately no easy way of assessing the age of a particular individual in most cases, and since Siamese fighting fish (*Betta splendens*) for example only live two to three years, then it may be advantageous, especially if you are hoping to breed your fish for exhibition purposes, to start out with individuals that are obviously not fully grown. Should you be interested in breeding a specific color strain or fin type, then it is not only the appearance of a particular fish that may be significant, but also its genetic ancestry. The records of a breeder can be important in this regard, helping to ensure that your pairings can be carried out to maximize the likelihood of developing the strain that appeals to you.

Most of the anabantoids that are generally available through aquatic stores have been bred on fish farms. Over successive generations, these fish have become adapted to environmental conditions that may not be the same as those encountered in their natural habitat. As a rule, those anabantoids that are widely available are likely to be among the easiest to keep successfully, as they are likely to be the most adaptable. Even so, some of the recently

● Some anabantoids, such as the Siamese fighting fish (*Betta splendens*), have been selectively bred for centuries. Their appearance has altered significantly as a result. The fish seen here is regarded as a wild-type example of the species.

discovered species are now being bred in increasing numbers, and provided that you can meet their water chemistry and other environmental needs, there is no reason why you cannot keep them with equal success.

MAKING A DECISION

Once you have decided on the fish that appeal to you, ask for them to be caught, so you can make a final check on them when they are in a plastic bag. This gives you a much better opportunity to study them at close quarters, to look for things like scale damage. Inspect the eyes closely as well, especially, because on occasions, some fish develop with just a single eye on their head, and this deformity may not be immediately obvious in the tank itself, especially among a group of fish.

It is usual for the transportation bags to be sealed with relatively little water and filled up with oxygen. Anabantoids in particular travel well in these surroundings since they can breathe air. The way that the bags are transported is important. It is far less stressful for the fish if these clear plastic bags are placed in paper bags before you leave—this means that male Siamese fighting fish (*Betta splendens*) won't be able to see each other for the duration of the journey, which would cause them to challenge each other throughout. Other anabantoids are also calmer transported in the dark.

Aim to take the fish home without delay, being careful to ensure that they are not placed in direct sunlight, as this can prove fatal surprisingly quickly due to excess temperature. The bags should be positioned so that they cannot tip over and so that other objects cannot fall on them. Do not place the fish in the trunk of the car, because the temperature may be much hotter or colder than in the car itself.

When you do arrive home, allow the water temperature in the bag to equilibrate with that in the tank, by allowing the bag to float for 15–20 minutes on the surface of the water. It is then a good idea to catch and release the fish with a net, rather than simply tipping them with the water in the bag into the aquarium, because this increases the risk of introducing harmful microbes into the tank at the outset.

Anabantoids generally do not like bright lighting conditions, so keep the aquarium lights off for a day, so that they can settle down. Otherwise, they may become nervous, even attempting to leap out of their quarters and collide with the aquarium hood as a result. Similarly, they are unlikely to start feeding at once, so it may be better to wait until the next day before offering them food. If it is left uneaten, this will start to decay in the tank before the filter is working effectively, causing a deterioration in water quality.

CLASSIFICATION

The way anabantoids are classified serves not only to reveal their associations with other types of fish, but also highlights closer relationships between members of this particular suborder. The classification system operates through a series of divisions called ranks, which become increasingly specific as one passes down through them. Taxonomy is a dynamic science though, and changes to the arrangement do occur on occasions. This area of zoology is likely to undergo even more radical alterations in the near future, as the result of DNA investigations, which enable relationships to be closely defined by biochemical means, rather than simply on anatomical grounds.

● The relationship between the different bushfish is a controversial area in anabantoid taxonomy. This is the blunt-headed bushfish (*Ctenopoma petherici*), which varies significantly in appearance across its range in western parts of Africa.

Traditional thinking on the taxonomy of anabantoids sees the five families in this book classified within the suborder Anabantoidei. In some cases, the family itself may be split into subfamilies, with the genera being grouped together beneath this heading, as set out below:

SUBORDER: Anabantoidei
Family: Anabantidae
Genera: *Anabas; Ctenopoma; Microctenopoma*

Family: Belontiidae
Subfamily: Belontiinae
Genus: *Belontia*

Subfamily: Macropodinae
Genera: *Betta; Ctenops; Macropodus; Malpulutta; Parosphromenus; Pseudosphromenus; Trichopsis*

Subfamily: Trichogasterinae
Genera: *Colisa*;
Parasphaerichthys;
Sphaerichthys; *Trichogaster*

Family: Helostomatidae
Genus: *Helostoma*

Family: Luciocephalidae
Genus: *Luciocephalus*

Family: Osphronemidae
Genus: *Osphronemus*

At least, that's how most stores and fish keepers see it at the moment! In fact, recently the chocolate gourami *(Sphaerichthys osphronemoides)*, *Luciocephalus*, *Ctenops*, *Colisa*, and *Trichogaster* have been placed in a new subfamily, Luciocephalinae, partly based on egg structure. For convenience we have stayed with the old divisions.

HOW THE SYSTEM WORKS

Family names always end in the letters -idae, whereas subfamily endings are -inae. Lower down, all ranks at and below generic level are written in italics, with the name of the genus always placed first, starting with a capital letter. A species is described by a combination of its generic name and its own specific name. Although in many cases, the species marks the lowest rank in the taxonomic tree, there are occasions when this description is further subdivided into subspecies or races.

A typical example of classification in action for the combtail is as follows:

Family: Belontiidae
Subfamily: Belontiinae
Genus: *Belontia*
Species: *Belontia signata*
Subspecies: *Belontia signata signata, Belontia signata jonklaasi*

The differences in appearance between subspecies are usually slight, but consistent. The subspecies for which the specific epithet is repeated, being *B. s. signata* in this case, is known as the nominate subspecies, meaning that it was the first to be discovered. It does not mean that it is the most common form.

◐ Slight consistent differences in appearance result in the recognition of subspecies, which represent the lowest order in the taxonomic tree. This is the pectoral spot combtail, known as *Belontia signata jonklaasi*, distinguishable by the dark spot on each side of its body, at the base of the pectoral fin.

The emergence of a color morph does not immediately lead to the creation of a new subspecies, rather this is usually indicated by the addition of the description "var.," meaning variant, at the end of the species' name, as in *Belontia signata* var. "Kottawa Forest," with this particular population of fish having distinctive coloration. Further study of wild variants may ultimately lead to them becoming recognized as subspecies in due course.

The naming process depends on a description of a specimen being published in a peer-reviewed publication, and the specimen used for this purpose, dubbed the so-called "type specimen" is then stored for future reference as part of a museum collection. This means that it can take some time between a previously unrecognized anabantoid being reported, and official recognition being accorded to it in the scientific literature. This has been particularly significant as far as bettas (*Betta* spp.) are concerned, because of the relatively large number of new species that were discovered during the last two decades of the 20th century.

⬇ Both the scientific name and the common name of a fish may signify its particular features, as in the case of the thick-lipped gourami (*Colisa labiosa*).

When changes to the classification of a particular species occur, this is indicated by the placing of the name of the person who is credited with first recording the species in parentheses, after its name. As an example, the climbing perch is now described under its contemporary name, written up as *Anabas testudineus* (Bloch, 1795), revealing that it has been reclassified since it was first recorded by Bloch. Where no change in nomenclature has occurred, as with the Siamese fighting fish, there is no use of brackets, with the styling in this case being *Betta splendens* Regan, 1909. The date after the person's name indicates the year in which the description was published, enabling newly discovered species to be differentiated from those that have been documented for centuries.

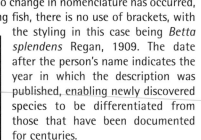

The scientific name is unique throughout the entire animal kingdom, so there should be no confusion over the identity of a particular fish. The choice of name may also give insights into the color, temperament, size, or shape of the fish. The characteristic feature of the thick-lipped gourami is reflected in its scientific name, *Colisa labiosa*, with "*labiosa*" referring to its lips.

ASIAN LABYRINTH FISH
FAMILY BELONTIIDAE

SUBFAMILY BELONTIINAE

Belontia

This genus comprises two species that can grow to a relatively large size, reaching 7.5in (19cm) in the larger honeycombed combtail (*B. hasselti*). It is the more widely distributed member of the group, ranging across the Malay Peninsula to islands in the region including Sumatra and Borneo, whereas the combtail (*B. signata*) itself is restricted just to Sri Lanka. In terms of their shape, combtails are sometimes confused with cichlids, partly as a result of the broadest part of their body being just behind the head rather than farther back toward the tail, as with many anabantoids. The name "combtail" is derived from the way in which the rays of the caudal fin project out from beyond the membrane like the teeth of a comb.

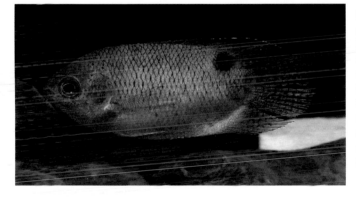

◐ A honeycombed combtail (*Belontia hasselti*). These fish often rest at strange angles against rockwork and other tank decor, which might suggest they are ill, but this is normal behavior in this species.

These anabantoids are not suitable for housing with smaller companions as they are predatory by nature. In addition, they are also aggressive toward each other, especially when spawning, and should only be mixed with suitably robust fish of similar size. Combtails tend to inhabit relatively fast-flowing stretches of water, and therefore have quite small, underdeveloped labyrinth organs, although on occasion, they rely on this organ to assist their respiration.

Active during the day, it is not uncommon for these fish to lay in an immobile state on the floor of their aquarium during periods of darkness. The breeding habits of combtails are less fixed than some members of this group of fish. They may not always construct a

The magnificent finnage is a feature of the male Siamese fighting fish (*Betta splendens*). As it is the best-known member of its genus, it is often simply called the betta in North America.

bubblenest of any type, but if they do this will only be built after mating has occurred. Their eggs float up to the surface and are quite large, measuring up to 0.05in (1.5mm) in diameter. Females may produce as many as 7,000 at a single spawning, with their partners then carrying the eggs elsewhere in their mouths if danger threatens, suggesting some links with mouthbrooding anabantoids.

SUBFAMILY MACROPODINAE

Betta

It is hard to determine the number of species that form this popular genus, partly because of taxonomic disagreements over existing species and also because of the discovery of a significant number of new members of this group. Almost certainly there will be others that will be added to the list in the future as well, particularly from lesser studied localities such as Borneo. Another problem is the way in which species have been translocated by people in the region, to the extent that these fish, especially the Siamese fighting fish (*B. splendens*) can be found well outside what may originally have been a fairly localized area of distribution.

The genus as a whole is represented across much of Southeast Asia and adjacent islands, extending as far south as Java. Within the group, however, there is a characteristic difference in appearance, which reflects a key distinction in their breeding habits. Although all species lay eggs, males of bubblenest-building species have smaller heads than those that are mouthbrooders; obviously the developing brood needs space within the oral cavity for its development. Males of mouthbrooding species which undertake this task therefore have a head shape that is proportionately longer than that of their bubblenesting counterparts.

There is also a significant difference in the number of eggs produced, with mouthbrooding species having fewer offspring, thanks to the greater security of being able to rear them through the critical early stages of life.

It appears that it may well have been the natural environment in which the fish are found that was originally responsible for shaping their reproductive behavior and hence their anatomical appearance. Bubblenesting bettas are to be found predominantly in still stretches of water where the flow rate of the water is negligible. On the other hand, their mouthbrooding relatives are to be found in faster-flowing streams and similar locations where the fragile nature of the bubblenest would be destroyed by the current. This division is not necessarily always clear-cut, since in some areas, both bubblenesting and mouthbrooding bettas can be found in the same stretch of water.

There is also an important secondary difference in appearance between mouthbrooding and bubblenesting bettas, with males of the latter group being significantly more colorful in appearance. This can be correlated with a more aggressive nature, and may reflect the need of these fish to compete for the best anchorage sites for their nests, whereas mouthbrooding bettas can occupy any stretch of water while waiting for their offspring to hatch. Male mouthbrooders are relatively nonaggressive by nature, except for the period around spawning itself. Nevertheless, if a group is housed together, it is not uncommon for the subdominant males to

🔽 The dimidiata dwarf mouthbrooder (*Betta dimidiata*) is, as its name suggests, one of the smaller mouthbrooding rather than bubblenesting members of its genus, growing to a maximum length of about 2.75in (7cm).

① Schaller's mouthbrooder (*Betta schalleri*). The coloration of mouthbrooding bettas is generally less flamboyant than that of their egg-laying relatives.

resemble females in appearance, with only the dominant male assuming full breeding coloration at this stage.

It can be quite difficult to distinguish between the sexes of mouthbrooding species, especially outside the breeding period, and their relatively plain appearance has counted against them, in terms of their aquarium popularity. It is no coincidence that the most colorful members of this genus, such as the Siamese fighting fish (*B. splendens*) have become more popular, although in theory at least, they may be harder to breed than the mouthbrooding species. This has not necessarily proved to be the case in practice, simply because their reproductive needs are now well understood, whereas those of the mouthbrooding species have yet to be scrutinized in such detail.

One aspect of their breeding behavior, which is common to both bubblenesting and mouthbrooding bettas, is the way their eggs sink, rather than float. This may help to explain why females are often involved in collecting the eggs after spawning, as it reduces the likelihood of them being lost. There is also a less obvious yet critical aspect to the development of the fry in the nest. They must be held in the nest up until the stage that they become free-swimming, because otherwise, they will be carried away in the water, lessening their chances of survival.

In the mouthbrooding bettas, the female usually helps to collect the eggs, spitting them out in front of the male's face, allowing him to take them into his mouth. An exception is the one-spot mouthbrooder (*B. unimaculata*) from northern Borneo, with reports suggesting that the male alone collects the eggs after spawning occurs.

Male mouthbrooding bettas usually remain close to the surface of the water, hanging in a distinctive pose with their heads held upwards at an angle, until the young hatch and become free-swimming. Although hatching typically occurs after about four days, the young fish will not leave the relative safety of the male's mouth until about a week after egg-laying occurred.

Ctenops

The Indian gourami (*C. nobilis*) is a monotypic genus, meaning that it is the only member of the group. It is actually little known and not widely kept in the aquarium hobby. These fish have a characteristic body shape, with a decidedly pointed snout. The dorsal fin is quite small, and is located in close proximity to the caudal fin. In terms of coloration, they are fairly drab, being predominantly brownish, aside from some silvery stripes running down the side of the body, although some individuals are of a darker, blackish shade. The sexes can be distinguished quite easily, since males have a narrow red edging to their caudal and anal fins. Regarded as closely related to members of the *Trichopsis* genus, the Indian gourami grows to a similar length, up to 4in (10cm).

The dull patterning of these fish helps to hide their presence, and makes them ideally suited to being an ambush predator, bearing some similarities in appearance to the leaf fish (*Monocirrhus polyacanthus*) of South America. They snap at any small aquatic creatures that come within reach and can be swallowed whole. In aquarium surroundings, it is essential to match the size of the Indian gourami's food to that of its jaws.

Unfortunately, their predatory diet based on invertebrates has left these fish vulnerable to acquiring metacercariae, which are the immature stage in the lifecycle of flukes, present in the bodies of their prey in the wild. This helps to explain why the species has been difficult to establish in the past, because in such cases the adult fish are weakened by this infection. Since these parasites have a complex lifecycle, however, they cannot be transmitted directly between fish but need to pass through an invertebrate host, so young tank-bred Indian gouramis should be free from this infection.

Although initially thought to be a bubblenesting species, the Indian gourami has now been confirmed as a mouthbrooder, which helps to explain its long jaws. The young undergo a sequence of color changes as they grow older, starting with the appearance of

⬆ Indian gourami
(*Ctenops nobilis*).
Floating plants are
recommended in an
aquarium housing
these anabantoids,
which tend to live
close to the water's
surface.

a broad beige band just behind the head. In spite of their lack of bright coloration, these gouramis have proved to be highly aggressive toward each other, and must be housed to reduce their belligerent behavior. Aside from ensuring that they are not overcrowded, these fish need to be kept in a well planted tank, where there are plenty of retreats available. They can become extremely territorial, even to the extent of not venturing out from a chosen area in the tank, where they will then need to be fed.

A water temperature between 71–77°F (22–25°C) is recommended, with neutral water conditions appearing to suit these unusual gouramis well. The addition of a little marine salt, at a rate of just one teaspoonful per 5.3gal (20 liters) can be beneficial, especially for combating potential fungal infections in recently acquired individuals.

Macropodus

This genus includes the hardiest of all the anabantoids, the paradisefish (*M. opercularis*), which is believed to have been the first member of the entire group brought to Europe. The natural range of *Macropodus* paradisefish extends across much of eastern and southeastern Asia, ranging from Korea as far south as Vietnam, as well as some offshore islands, although their precise natural distribution is unclear, as they may have been translocated in the past. Certainly, it is believed that the populations of paradisefish occurring on the Ryuku Islands of Japan, marking the northerly border of their range, were introduced there, as were populations on Borneo.

Paradisefish have proved to be remarkably adaptable, with *M. chinensis* for example being capable of surviving at temperatures as low as 40°F (5°C) during the winter period. They can even breed successfully in water at a temperature of just 68°F (20°C), although this dramatically slows the development of the young fry. In any event, brood care is often quite protracted in these fish, and unusually, the female may play a role, even in the absence of the male. They lay large numbers of eggs that float in the water and need to be steered into the bubblenest, which is constructed by the male.

The adaptability of these fish is further emphasized by the presence of a highly efficient labyrinth organ, which enables them to live under conditions that would be fatal for other fish. Paradisefish can continue breathing when the irrigation ditches in which they may be found turn into little more than muddy puddles during dry periods. Their survival is also assisted by their adaptable feeding habits, with the natural diet of paradisefish being comprised of a wide variety of aquatic invertebrates. They tend to hunt near the surface for their food, snapping at any creatures that come within reach, and hence they have been thought to be valuable for destroying mosquitoes.

In areas where the distribution of the different species overlaps, there is a risk that they may hybridize. The markings of the fish appear to prevent hybridization, however, as shown by studies involving paradisefish (*M. opercularis*) and black paradisefish (*M. concolor*). Pairings of a male black paradisefish with an ordinary female paradisefish are believed not to be successful on the basis that the male fish lacks the distinctive blue spot on the gill covers, so the female fish fails to recognize her would-be partner.

There are some taxonomists who favor the grouping of these two species together, regarding them as subspecies. Where the pairing is reversed, so the spotting is not an issue, and successful hybridization occurs, then their offspring are generally fertile, suggesting a close relationship between these forms in spite of the anatomical distinctions separating these fish. It is not always easy

🠕 The attractively patterned paradise-fish (*Macropodus opercularis*) ranks among the hardiest of all anabantoids. The yellow form (left) is commonly but inaccurately called the albino.

open, clear stretches of flowing water where oxygen levels are generally good and so they rarely need to surface to breathe air. All species appear to be bubblenest builders, in spite of their size and that they live in flowing waters that would destroy any attempt to build a bubblenest at the surface. Instead, the male chooses a nest site in a sheltered area under the surface of the water, in a small cave for example, which they can occupy without difficulty because of their small size. The eggs may even adhere here on their own, especially where the water is soft, in the absence of a proper bubblenest.

Once spawning has occurred, the male drives off the female and guards the nest on his own. In spite of their small size, the development of both the eggs and the resulting fry is slower than that of other anabantoids. Hatching alone takes three days at a temperature of 77°F (25°C). At this stage, the young still have a large yolk sac and so it takes a further four to six days before they are free-swimming. By this stage, they are about 0.25in (5mm) in length and can be reared on brine shrimp nauplii, although some infusoria at this early stage is often beneficial.

Parosphromenus gouramis can prove to be prolific. An experiment to investigate the dependence of *P. deisneri* on atmospheric air (which entailed depriving a pair of access to the water's surface over a period of more than 100 days), saw the pair spawn approximately every 10 days on average during this period. They can typically produce between 10 and 40 offspring at a single spawning. For breeding purposes, pairs need to be housed on their own, but they are not aggressive fish by nature and are sometimes encountered in groups in the wild. There must be caves for each fish to use as a retreat, but outside these areas, they will not prove to be territorial by nature. These gouramis thrive in soft, slightly acidic water that is well-filtered to replicate the flowing waters they inhabit in the wild.

The *Parosphromenus* genus offers great scope for the specialist gourami breeder, partly thanks to the small size of these fish, which means that pairs do not require spacious accommodation. Subdued lighting, dense planting and good water quality are all essential to their well-being in aquarium surroundings. It may be possible to wean them on to flaked food, although small live foods are invariably preferred.

Pseudosphromenus

The two members of this genus are commonly called spiketails, because of the long projections present in the center of their caudal fins. They are found in a wide range of different habitats, even being encountered in brackish waters in some cases. They are also surprisingly adaptable in terms of water temperatures. In Sri Lanka, Day's spiketail (*P. dayi*) has been recorded in mountain streams, where the temperature can be as low as 60°F (16°C), while elsewhere on the island this species has been found in lowland areas in waters as warm as 92°F (34°C). Field observations suggest that spiketails occurring in the highlands, where the flow rate is significantly higher, do not construct a bubblenest of any type, unlike their lowland counterparts but simply spawn on plants, rocks, and the base of the stream.

Distinguishing the sexes outside the spawning period can be problematic, but males become more colorful in appearance at this stage, while females in comparison turn significantly darker. Otherwise, it may be possible to identify females by their more rotund shape, especially when the fish are viewed from above. Older individuals of the red-eyed spiketail (*Pseudosphromenus cupanus*) can be identified, as they lose the darker spot which is present on the caudal peduncle.

🔽 Day's spiketail (*Pseudosphromenus dayi*). The characteristic projections may be less conspicuous if these fish have been housed under less than ideal conditions, but they can regrow subsequently.

In aquarium surroundings, the bubblenest is constructed below the surface of the water, and a cave should be incorporated along with plants for this purpose. The female as well as the male often protect the eggs, and then the fry. The water temperature has a marked effect on the length of time it takes for the eggs to hatch. This effectively doubles from just 30 hours at 77°F (25°C) to about 60 hours at 73°F (23°C). Young spiketails lack the characteristic tail shape seen in adult fish, with this feature not developing until they are approaching 1in (2.5cm) in length.

Both species are easy to keep and make an ideal introduction to the anabantoid group, as they can be persuaded to spawn quite easily, as well as being quite peaceful by nature. They should not be housed together, because they hybridize readily, and there are reports that suggest their offspring are fertile.

⬆ The calls of the croaking gourami (*Trichopsis vittatus*) are likely to be made with greater frequency when the fish are in spawning condition.

Trichopsis

There is some dispute among taxonomists about the relationships of the gouramis that form this genus. Three species are generally recognized, although they hybridize together readily and produce fertile offspring, like *Pseudosphromenus*. Furthermore, the wide range of the croaking gourami itself (*T. vittatus*) across much of Southeast Asia has meant that it occurs in a number of recognizable forms, some of which have been accorded specific status in the past because of their divergence in appearance.

One of the most distinctive patterns is seen in croaking gouramis from Thailand, which have just three horizontal black stripes extending along their bodies, and a well-defined black spot located just behind the gill plates on each side of the body. In other cases the stripes are broken up into a more generalized spotted patterning running down the body, creating a different appearance. Others may display large double spots, while there is also a blue-colored variant, known as blue croaking gourami and often recognized as a separate species, under the description of *Trichopsis harrisi*. These variations are less apparent in aquarium strains, as they have been commercially bred over generations, resulting in more standardized markings.

The reason for the natural divergence in the appearance of these gouramis is their distribution. Not only are there a number of island populations, but in addition, those occurring on the mainland may be found isolated in particular stretches of water. This is because of the geography of the terrain in which these fish occur, with the presence of mountain ranges through the region serving as an impenetrable barrier to their movements.

It is no coincidence that even widely distributed mammalian and avian species in the Indo-Malayan region occur in a number of distinctive forms, as the result of isolation, and they are obviously far less constrained by their environment than fish. These geographical barriers in effect predispose ultimately to the creation of new species, as the resulting isolated populations are increasingly shaped by the selection pressures within their restricted ranges. It may be that this has occurred already, as it would explain the creation of fertile hybrids between the three recognized *Trichopsis* species, which suggests a close biological relationship between them, since most hybrids are sterile.

Croaking gouramis generally inhabit waters that are not only slow flowing, but also cloudy, so the visibility is extremely poor. This may have led to the development of their distinctive calls, which are most audible at the time for spawning, when pairs need to locate each other. Females of this genus are unusual in that they do not release their eggs individually, but rather produce them in distinct clusters. Again, this may be a behavior pattern linked to living in murky waters, where it would be hard to locate loose eggs in the environment. Each cluster is typically comprised of as many as six eggs, and if they do break up, then both adult fish seek to find the eggs and transfer them to their nest. This is well-anchored to floating plants, or sometimes to rockwork.

It is not always easy to recognize the sexes when these gouramis are young, although if the females are viewed with a light from behind, then their yellowish-colored ovaries should be apparent through their flanks, below the swim bladder. The dorsal and anal fins are typically larger in mature male fish, especially croaking gouramis (*T. vittatus*) themselves. These fins continue growing well into maturity, so that older individuals can be clearly recognized by this characteristic.

SUBFAMILY TRICHOGASTERINAE

Colisa

The four species comprising this genus, along with those forming the *Trichogaster* genus, differ from other anabantoids because of the long, threadlike appearance of their pelvic fins. These typically reach back to the level of the caudal fin. This feature has led to them being called threadfish. It is easy to distinguish the *Colisa* species because their dorsal and anal fins are of approximately similar length, in contrast to *Trichogaster* where the dorsal fin is much shorter, and there is also no sign of the forking of the

🔽 The dwarf gourami (*Colisa lalia*) is a popular and widely kept species.

caudal fin itself. Young dwarf gouramis (*C. lalia*) can be sexed with relative ease since, even at an early stage, females have rounded rather than pointed dorsal fins.

With a distribution centered on the Indian subcontinent, the range of *Colisa* species in the wild nevertheless shows marked seasonal changes. Following the start of the monsoon period in July, which heralds heavy rainfall, these gouramis extend their range out into the shallow floodplains where breeding can occur, right through until October. Then as the water level starts to fall, so they move back into the rivers, with their growing young congregating together in schools. Within the aquarium therefore, significant water changes coupled with an increasing percentage of live food in the diet, to mimic the effects of the rains, should help to trigger spawning behavior.

🔼 A number of different variants of the dwarf gourami (*Colisa lalia*) exist, some of which are the result of hybridization. This particular individual belongs to the so-called Calcutta strain.

A potential problem is that male *Colisa* gouramis, which become much more colorful in appearance at this stage, are unusually determined when courting. It is essential that the females have adequate retreats in their quarters, to prevent them suffering loss of condition as the result of persistent harassment from would-be mates. Even so, these gouramis are justifiably popular, not only because of their attractive coloration, but also because they can be housed easily as part of a community aquarium in the company of companions of similar size.

Color variants are not unusual among members of this genus, with the most common ones seen in the aquarium hobby being the result of hybridization. In other cases, as with the giant gourami (*C. fasciata*), a number of localized forms have been recorded, reflecting the isolated distribution of a number of populations of this

fish—however, these individual variations tend to be lost as the result of domestication for the aquatic trade.

There have been blue and red varieties of dwarf gouramis (*C. lalia*) available since the early 1980s, but they have not proved easy to establish. It has been suggested that at least some of the early red varieties were developed by color feeding, as their coloration subsequently became duller with time. There is also evidence based on breeding studies, however, that some of these fish are the result of a genetic change, with red coloration being due to an autosomal recessive mutation (*see* pages 99–100).

Most of the red-colored fish that have been available have been males, and have had to be paired with normal females. As would be expected from the genetics of this pairing, all the resulting offspring resemble normal dwarf gouramis in color. Yet when these are paired together, approximately a quarter of each brood then comprises red-colored fish, confirming the genetic nature of this color change. This particular variety, with its contrasting blue dorsal fin, is known as the neon. Hybridized varieties are more likely to be infertile.

Female *Colisa* gouramis are normally quite prolific, producing hundreds of eggs, but rearing is not always straightforward because their fry rank among the smallest of all anabantoids. They must therefore be provided with correspondingly fine particles of food such as rotifers through the critical early stages of life, once they become free-swimming.

⬆ In spite of its name, this so-called giant gourami (*Colisa fasciata*) is actually tiny when compared with the true giant gourami (see page 47), attaining a maximum size of just under 5in (12cm).

● This is the crossband race of the chocolate gourami known as *Sphaerichthys osphromenoides selatanensis*. The depth of the chocolate coloration of these fish can alter dramatically, depending on their environmental conditions.

The size of the bubblenest is influenced by the gouramis' environment. Where there is a dense covering of vegetation on the surface of the water, the male fish build a bubblenest that may be 1in (2.5cm) in depth, but if there is less cover available, the nest itself is likely to be larger, but not as deep. This may not only help to give the structure more stability, but could also serve to protect the contents of the nest more effectively from predators. Some male dwarf gouramis (*C. lalia*) may even collect pieces of vegetation which they incorporate into the nest, presumably affording it greater strength and camouflage.

Parasphaerichthys

The sole member of this genus is known as the Burmese or false chocolate gourami (*P. ocellatus*), being identifiable by its narrower, more elongated body shape. These gouramis can grow up to approximately 2.5in (6cm), but are usually smaller in size, and display a variable orange-yellow and brownish patterning over their bodies, which enables individuals to be told apart at a glance.

Originating from mountain streams in the northern part of Myanmar (Burma), near the Indawggyi and Inle lakes, the false chocolate gourami was first described in 1929. As a result of the inaccessibility of its native habitat, this species then remained unknown in aquarist circles until the early 1980s, when a few of these fish were brought alive to Europe for the first time.

False chocolate gouramis are shy by nature, and should be housed in a well-planted tank, which incorporates plenty of retreats. Floating plants and subdued lighting are likely to reduce their nervousness. Soft water conditions, combined with a pH between slightly acid and neutral are essential. A water temperature in the range of 72–77°F (22–25°C) suits them well. No breeding records appear to exist, but it is suspected that these particular gouramis are mouthbrooders.

Sphaerichthys

The three members of this genus occur much farther southeast in Asia, compared with *Parasphaerichthys*, although their exact range, especially in the case of the chocolate gourami (*S. osphromenoides*) itself, is still unclear. The largest member of the group is the pointed-mouth chocolate gourami (*S. acrostoma*), which can grow to 2.8in (7cm) overall. *Sphaerichthys* gouramis all tend to be found in relatively shallow, slow-flowing stretches of water, where the conditions may sometimes be sufficiently acidic and the mineral levels so low as to curb plant growth.

If kept in correspondingly soft and acidic water conditions in aquarium surroundings, these gouramis can be maintained quite satisfactorily, with the addition of aquarium peat to the filter assisting in this regard. Nevertheless, they do have a reputation for being rather delicate, partly because they are sensitive to any buildup of nitrate in the water. In addition, they appear particularly vulnerable to skin parasites such as *Oodinium*.

When frightened, the distinctive coloration of chocolate gouramis lightens considerably, as is likely to occur on the ride home after purchase. This change is only temporary however, being reversed once the gouramis are settled in their new surroundings. The nervous side to their nature can then be partly overcome by a careful choice of bolder yet nonaggressive tankmates, with red rasboras or harlequins (*Rasbora heteromorpha*) being recommended for this purpose, as they thrive under similar water conditions.

Controversy has surrounded the breeding habits of chocolate gouramis in the past, but they are now regarded as mouthbrooders, with the female undertaking this task. Interestingly, there are reports that some bubbles are blown out of the mouth soon after spawning has occurred, and females do not gather their eggs up immediately either. Furthermore, the number of eggs produced exceeds the space available to accommodate them in the female's mouth—all these observations suggest that these particular anabantoids still retain vestigial behavioral signs of a recent bubble-nesting past.

Trichogaster

Although superficially similar in appearance to *Colisa* species, with threadlike pelvic fins, members of the *Trichogaster* genus are significantly larger. Close examination reveals that these fins are different in structure too, being formed of two fin rays fused together. The color differences between the sexes is less marked in *Trichogaster* gouramis than their *Colisa* cousins, but sexing is straightforward, on the basis of the shape of the dorsal fin, which is significantly longer and tapers to a point in mature males. It normally extends back as far as the caudal fin, whereas it usually only reaches to the caudal peduncle in females. Females also tend to be slightly smaller in size and have a more rounded body shape.

The distribution of the four *Trichogaster* species occurs farther east than their *Colisa* relatives, and is centered on Southeast Asia and nearby offshore islands including Borneo. The largest member of the group is the snakeskin gourami (*T. pectoralis*), which can reach 8in (20cm) in length. Nevertheless, thanks to their relatively small mouths, they require small items of food, readily taking brine shrimp nauplii, as well as flake food, in preference to other larger food items. They also nibble at plants, including algae, which can make them valuable in an aquarium to help keep such growth under control.

Trichogaster gouramis rank among the most popular of all anabantoids in the aquarium hobby, not only because of the relative ease with which they can be kept but also thanks to the significant number of attractive color varieties that have been created. Some are the result of selective breeding of natural color variants, whereas others have been bred by hybridization. Among the most popular forms are golden varieties of both the pearl gourami (*T. leeri*) and the spotted gourami (*T. trichopterus*), and assorted blue-colored varieties, notably in the latter species. These are derived essentially from the blue Sumatran subspecies (*T. t. sumatranus*).

In the wild, male *Trichogaster* gouramis seek out still areas of water for breeding purposes. Here they can anchor their bubblenests between the leaves of plants growing on the surface. All species, with the exception of the moonbeam gourami (*T. microlepis*), do not use

◐ Pearl gouramis (*Trichogaster leeri*) are so called because of their distinctive white spots. They are sometimes referred to as lace, or mosaic, gouramis. They are a great starter fish; every home should have one!

any pieces of vegetation directly as a means of providing additional support in the construction of their nests.

Female *Trichogaster* gouramis take the initiative in the courtship process, seeking out males under their bubblenests. During spawning embraces, they can produce up to 80 eggs at a time, with a typical spawning often consisting of 1,000 eggs or more in total. These float up into the nest and hatch within two days, depending on the water temperature. It has become clear from breeding these gouramis in aquarium surroundings that the subsequent growth of the fry is not consistent, as some grow at a significantly faster rate than others.

This discrepancy, presumably mediated through differing outputs or responses to growth hormone, could bring some survival benefits, as it means there is less pressure on the available food supply. Furthermore, if the water level falls significantly, then the smaller individuals may be able to survive better than their larger companions.

As far as aquarium stocks are concerned, those young gouramis that are growing more slowly should be separated out from their faster-developing siblings, and then reared separately. *Trichogaster* gouramis in general are not aggressive fish, which is another reason for their popularity among aquarium keepers. Although adult individuals may bully any significantly smaller companions sharing their quarters, they are generally tolerant of each other and of other fish of similar size.

◑ The Sumatran race of the spotted gourami (*Trichogaster trichopterus sumatranus*) is characterized by its intense blue coloration, often being described simply as the blue gourami.

FAMILY HELOSTOMATIDAE

Helostoma

The popular kissing gourami (*H. temminckii*) is the only member of this family. It has an extensive distribution across Southeast Asia where it is popular as a source of food. Indeed, it has been so widely translocated through the range that the locality where these fish originated is unclear. Certainly, the kissing gourami is a highly adaptable species, occurring in a wide range of environments from lakes to rivers. There is a significant difference in appearance between the wild form, which is a silvery-gray shade overall with more iridescent greenish markings on the sides of the body, and the domesticated form that is popular with aquarium keepers. These fish are whitish overall, usually with a slight pinkish or yellowish hue to their bodies.

Although kissing gouramis can grow to approximately 12in (30cm) in the wild, they are unlikely to reach more than half this length in

● The kissing gourami (*Helostoma temminckii*). Sexing of these particular gouramis by visual means is virtually impossible, especially outside the spawning period.

the aquarium. They can be bred here though, although sexing the pale domesticated color morph is difficult, because the characteristic changes seen in the male in the wild form do not become so clearly evident. Normally, their dorsal and anal fins turn darker at this stage, while their body becomes more colorful.

Live food is an important trigger for breeding these gouramis, and as the time for spawning approaches, so the characteristic locking of their fleshy lips with each other is more likely to be observed. It is not a display of affection, but a test of strength. The fish may stay locked together for long periods. Their bulbous lips also help them to feed on algae, with rows of so-called "hip teeth" being present here for rasping purposes. Vegetable matter forms a significant part of their diet.

Unlike many members of the group, kissing gouramis do not build a bubblenest. Instead, their eggs simply float up to the surface

and stick to water plants there, thanks to their adhesive nature. As a prelude to mating, the pair again lock mouths, and may also anchor on to the sides of their partner's body in a similar fashion. Spawning often occurs from dusk onwards, which may mean that the eggs released by the female are less conspicuous to predators in the relative darkness. They can lay huge numbers of eggs, with over 10,000 sometimes being produced at a single spawning, making them among the most prolific of all gouramis.

In Thailand, where kissing gouramis are bred for food, pairs are kept apart for a time, so the female is ready to spawn almost instantly when she is introduced to her mate. The eggs are then frequently scooped off the surface and transferred to hatching quarters, where fine food particles are critical to the survival of the fry once they use up their yolk sac reserves, and become free-swimming.

⬆ As a predatory species, the pikehead (*Luciocephalus pulcher*) has a different body shape compared with that of other anabantoids.

FAMILY LUCIOCEPHALIDAE

Luciocephalus

Whereas kissing gouramis are effectively peaceful and partially vegetarian in their feeding habits, the pikehead (*L. pulcher*) is an aggressive predator, with a correspondingly large mouth to match, unlike that of most gouramis. Pikeheads do possess a labyrinth organ, although it has a more basic structure than that of other anabantoids. It may well be more important for improving the hearing of these fish, rather than serving primarily to assist their survival in poorly oxygenated water.

There are other anatomical differences as well, which have contributed to pikeheads being classified in a family on their own, including the fact that the first ray of their pelvic fin comprises a hard spine, whereas in other labyrinth fish, all the rays forming the structural support for this fin are soft. Their behavior is also significantly different. The pikehead's ambush technique of hunting prey is facilitated not only by its body shape, but also by its coloration. This varies significantly through its range, which extends right across the Malay

Peninsula to islands in the region, including Sumatra and Borneo, and presumably helps these fish to blend into their particular background. The pikehead's pattern of stripes augmented with spots, and neutral yellowish-brown body color serves to conceal its presence effectively, especially in among aquatic vegetation.

Their sleek, long torpedo-shape means they can accelerate quickly from rest. This propulsive thrust is assisted not only by the presence of a powerful caudal fin, but also by the proximity of the dorsal and the deeply notched anal fin. As a result, pikeheads, which are often encountered in groups, are well equipped to seize unsuspecting passing prey that swims too close to where an individual is lurking out of sight.

At close quarters, the unique anatomy of the pikehead's jawbones comes into play, being pushed forward to create a funnel though which smaller fish as well as invertebrates can literally be sucked directly into the mouth. Unfortunately, these fascinating fish are not easy to maintain in aquarium surroundings, partly because of their dietary needs. They are also able to jump up and seize insects that are just above the surface of the water. As a result, hatchling crickets sold for herptile food can be useful for these fish, particularly as their nutritional value can be enhanced by the use of a supplement (see page 87).

The pikehead was first described as long ago as 1830, and the earliest aquarium records for this species date back to 1905, although it has never been commonly available. It was assumed to be the only member not only of its genus, but also the family, right up until the late 1990s, when another species was found on Borneo, although its precise distribution here is presently unclear. It has been dubbed the spotted pikehead, being significantly different in appearance to its better-known relative. This fish has grayish upperparts, with a broad black band on each side of the body, spotted with yellow markings that extend on to the caudal fin, with the underparts being whitish, although it has still not been fully described scientifically at the time of writing.

It is similar in size to the pikehead itself, growing to about 8in (20cm) long. Spotted pikeheads have a similar profile, including the characteristically deep notched anal fin. They are believed to be mouthbrooders too, although there was initially confusion about the breeding habits of pikeheads. The presence of a number of small individuals in the early shipments received in the west from Asia led to the mistaken belief that these fish were actually livebearers. Only later, when their habits were studied more closely in aquarium surroundings did it become clear that eggs were laid by the female, and that the male subsequently brooded them in his mouth.

FAMILY OSPHRONEMIDAE

Osphronemus

This genus comprises what are potentially the largest of the ana-bantoids. The most common species, known simply as the giant gourami (*O. goramy*) has been documented as reaching up to 28in (70cm) in length on occasions, although sexual maturity is reached at a size of 5–7in (12–14cm). Although the giant gourami probably originated from the island of Java, it has been spread more widely through the Asian continent than any other fish, owing to its popularity as a source of food.

Unfortunately, their large size precludes adult giant gouramis from being kept satisfactorily in the home by all but the most dedicated enthusiast, although they are popular exhibits in public aquariums, and ideal for ponds in areas where the climate is suitably tropical. They can become quite tame in such surroundings, taking food from the hand in a similar way to koi.

It is important not to confuse the giant gourami with *Colisa fasciata*, which inappropriately shares this common name, although it only grows to a maximum size of approximately 4in (10cm) overall! Young giant gouramis do find their way into the

🔾 This particular species, known as the red-finned giant gourami (*Osphronemus laticlavius*) is one of the largest of all anabantoids, capable of growing to at least 20in (50cm) long.

● A number of different color forms have occurred of the giant gourami (*Osphronemus goramy*). This particular variety is known as the golden.

aquarium trade, although at this stage they differ significantly in appearance from that of adults. They have a decidedly elongated snout, with a flat top to the head. They are greenish-gray colored, with vertical stripes across the body and a dark spot with a yellow border on the caudal peduncle, so they can be confused with chocolate gouramis (*Sphaerichthys osphromenoides*).

As giant gouramis approach sexual maturity their head shape alters, becoming less elongated. The indented shape of the forehead is reversed, creating an obvious swelling on this part of the body, which will be especially evident in older male fish. The height of their body increases, so they appear taller and less streamlined. A noticeable change in color also results as they grow older, with giant gouramis turning gray and losing their striped appearance. The shape of the individual scales is then highlighted by darker gray edging, while their fins assume a greenish-blue shade. Sexing of mature fish is possible, thanks to the difference in appearance of the dorsal and anal fins, with those of males being longer at their tips, compared with the rounded outline characteristic of female giant gouramis.

Mature females have a huge reproductive potential, as befits their size, often laying 20,000 eggs or more at a single spawning. Their breeding behavior can be variable, as pairs sometimes use a floating bubblenest, or may alternatively prefer to use a cave beneath the surface. Under favorable conditions, young giant gouramis develop quickly, attaining sexual maturity in some cases by six months old, although they will continue growing after this stage, with larger fish tending to produce bigger broods.

The rearing quarters for giant gouramis need to be suitably spacious. They can be fed a significant amount of plant matter in their diet, with corresponding large food sticks or pellets being ideal for those housed in aquarium surroundings. It can be difficult to house them in planted aquariums since they often destroy the vegetation by eating it.

As with other gouramis that are bred widely, a golden color variant of the giant gourami has become established. Young fish are particularly striking in this case, being predominantly lemony-white, with their yellow coloration usually most evident along the back. This deepens in older fish, to assume a more golden hue.

Having first been classified back in 1802, the giant gourami was believed to be the only member of its genus right through until the 1990s, when a further two species, both from Borneo, were identified. The sevenstripe giant gourami (*O. scptcmfasciatus*) is distinguished on the basis of its striped patterning running down the sides of the body, which is retained in adult fish. The second new species is the red-finned giant gourami (*O. laticlavius*), originating from Sabah in Borneo. Young red-fins are much lighter than adults, being primarily silvery in color, with a dark spot on each side of the caudal peduncle. Their appearance then alters dramatically as they age, and they become slate-gray overall, although there is a distinctive reddish suffusion to their fins, including the long pelvic fins. Both these species tend to grow to a slightly smaller size than the giant gourami, reaching a maximum length of about 20in (50cm). As yet, they are rare within the aquarium hobby.

● The albino form of the giant gourami (*Osphronemus goramy*) is characterized by its red eyes.

Other forms may yet wait to be discovered. A rare orange-headed giant gourami (tentatively described scientifically as *Osphronemus* cf. *gourami*) has been documented, and is distinguishable by the relative absence of dark pigmentation on the head in fish of both sexes. At present, its precise distribution appears unclear. It may be, of course, that these are localized variants which have developed as a result of the translocation of wild populations by people in the past. Such fish would then have been isolated, increasing the likelihood of particular features becoming established within the populations concerned. In fact, there is some disagreement as to whether the natural range of the giant gourami itself included Borneo, or whether it was introduced there.

ASIAN/AFRICAN LABYRINTH FISH

FAMILY ANABANTIDAE

Anabas

The members of this family are split in their distribution, with the majority occurring in Africa. The climbing perch (*A. testudineus*) is an exception, being found across much of southern Asia, making it the most wide-ranging of all labyrinth fish. It can be encountered from India eastward to the Philippines and Indonesia. It is suspected that its occurrence in some areas, especially on islands such as Taiwan, is the result of human interference rather than representing part of the species' natural range. Such movements are the result of its importance as a food fish.

Climbing perch are able to colonize new territories more effectively than most fish because they can live surprisingly well out of water for long periods, breathing air using their highly efficient labyrinth organs. The way in which the climbing perch hauls itself along on land has led to it being likened to a tortoise, hence "*testudineus*" as part of its scientific name. In spite of stories to the contrary, these fish must return to the water to feed, and they are true omnivores, with their adaptable feeding habits encouraging their spread. Although often predatory, they will move into flooded rice paddies and frequently feed on the grains of the cereal in these surroundings.

Not surprisingly, the climbing perch was one of the first tropical fish to be kept in Europe, being displayed at London Zoo as early as

⊕ The high-bodied climbing perch (*Anabas oligolepis*) is rarely seen in the aquarium hobby.

1870. Their ability to breathe atmospheric air and their remarkable adaptability in terms of water chemistry meant that they were able to survive the long sea journey from their Asiatic homeland without problems.

Although the climbing perch itself dominates aquarium literature, there is a second species, known as the high-bodied climbing perch (*A. oligolepis*), occurring in northeastern India and Bangladesh. It is similar in appearance, but close study reveals some anatomical differences. These include a taller body, with a different structure to the dorsal fin in terms of the spine and ray count, not to mention bigger and thus fewer scales covering the lateral line running down the side of the body. The high-bodied climbing perch is exceedingly rare within the aquarium hobby, and there do not appear to be any spawning records for this species. Nevertheless, its requirements probably do not differ significantly from those of its near relative. It too is sometimes encountered in brackish waters, but its preferred habitat appears to be well-vegetated ponds.

AFRICAN LABYRINTH FISH
Ctenopoma

● Banded bushfish (*Ctenopoma fasciolatum*). The behaviour of most *Ctenopoma* species is not well documented, as these fish are less commonly kept than Asiatic anabantoids.

All members of this relatively large genus are to be found in Africa south of the Sahara, and are associated with all the major river systems of the continent. The exact number of species in this genus is still unclear, especially as local variants in appearance are not uncommon, but there are probably 20 or so in total. In common with the Asiatic climbing perches, these fish all have serrations on their gill covers that can assist them to move out of water. The fact that they can be found on land is why their common name is bushfish.

A characteristic feature of the group is the presence of scales with spines, present behind the eyes and also sometimes on the caudal peduncle. The number of spines varies, and this has provided a means of distinguishing species that are believed to be closely related. They are to be seen only in male bushfish, helping to hold the pair together while mating takes place.

The reproductive habits of *Ctenopoma* species vary, with some being bubblenest builders, while others display no interest in their eggs after spawning. Those in the latter group are typically the larger members of the genus, growing up to 8in (20cm) overall. The smaller species such as the Congo bushfish (*C. congicum*), which average around 3in (7.5cm) are now sometimes separated into the genus *Microctenopoma*, reflecting their smaller size.

The diversity in the breeding habits of these labyrinth fish includes the spawning process itself. Some species, such as the Nile ctenopoma (*C. muriei*) spawn in schools, (*see* page 91) resulting with females mating with different males. Mating itself takes place when the female slows, allowing a male to catch up with her, and the nuptial embrace lasts literally just a few seconds, with up to 30 eggs being released on each occasion. This process takes place repeatedly, with a female producing anywhere from 200 to 2,000 eggs during the mating cycle.

African labyrinth fish are generally less well known in aquarist circles compared with those originating from Asia, in spite of their interesting behavior patterns. They are not commercially bred on the same scale, despite larger species being valued as a source of food. They are not generally as colorful as their Asiatic counterparts, which means that there is less demand for them as aquarium occupants. Many are dark, but there are some exceptions, such as the attractively colored orange bushfish (*C. ansorgii*), and the banded bushfish (*C. fasciolatum*) with its blue and white markings, while some populations of blunt-headed bushfish (*C. petherici*) from the vicinity of West Africa are distinctly silvery in appearance.

Bushfish are predatory, although their care is reasonably straightforward provided that any companions are chosen carefully. Members of the group often prove to be rather shy by nature, which means that they are not conspicuous aquarium occupants in a well-planted tank, with some *Ctenopoma* species believed to be primarily nocturnal. Yet for the specialist, keeping members of this group of African anabantoids represents a considerable opportunity to add to the rather limited knowledge currently available about their behavior.

◐ The orange bushfish (*Ctenopoma ansorgii*) is one of the more colorful members of its genus.

◖ The Cape perch (*Sandelia capensis*). This species is sexually mature at just 2in (5cm) long, although it will grow much larger.

Sandelia

The two *Sandelia* species are confined to a fairly limited area of South Africa. Both can grow to about 8in (20cm). Bain's perch (*S. bainsii*), also known as the rocky perch, has the most southerly distribution of any anabantoid, and is found close to East London and the surrounding area. It is brownish, with spots and stripes in younger individuals, and has a broad body with a large mouth. There is a pair of small spines on the gill covers, with the labyrinth organ being small and not highly developed. Its underdeveloped labyrinth—the result of evolving in relatively oxygen-rich water—has not helped the wild rocky in its struggle to survive. Damming and weed proliferation have reduced the water's oxygen content, and the rocky is listed by the IUCN as endangered. Captive-bred fish have been released to improve numbers. These are unsocial fish with a reputation for being extremely aggressive—they should never be kept with smaller companions. They are highly adaptable in their water chemistry requirements. A well-aerated aquarium with a strong power filter is recommended, replicating the currents encountered in the rivers where they occur.

The Cape perch or Cape kurper (*S. capensis*) inhabits river systems to the northeast of Cape Town, approximately 420 miles (700km) from its relative. It is predominantly grayish, often with a bluish hue. Younger individuals are typically more yellowish with stripes on the sides of their bodies.

As both members of this genus occur outside the tropics, the aquarium water temperature should be maintained between 64–72°F (18–22°C). Neither is commonly available to aquarium keepers in other parts of the world.

The breeding behavior of the Cape perch resembles some *Ctenopoma* species; the male does not construct a bubblenest, although unusually he guards the eggs after spawning. These are adhesive, and stick to nearby plants or rocks. Hatching takes less than two days at the upper end of the temperature range, with the young becoming free-swimming within a further 24 hours. They take brine shrimp nauplii once they are about eight days old.

CHAPTER 3

Characteristics and Care

Anabantoids as a group have become popular because not only can many species be housed successfully in a decorative community tank, alongside other fish, showing to good effect in these surroundings, but also because they offer plenty of scope for the specialist breeder and exhibitor.

ANABANTOID CHARACTERISTICS

It is quite hard to generalize about the appearance of anabantoids. Many gouramis tend to have relatively narrow bodies, especially in those species occurring in heavily vegetated waters. This may enable them to swim more freely in these surroundings, where movement is easily restricted. Bettas, however, which are generally smaller in size, have a more rotund shape.

The shape and positioning of the dorsal fin in particular is variable in members of this group. It may be long and relatively low in height, running down much of the length of the back, as in *Colisa* species, or shorter and taller in appearance, as typified by members

of the *Parosphromenus* genus. The length of this fin can also serve to distinguish the sexes, as can the caudal fin. This is forked and elongated at its tips in the male black paradisefish (*Macropodus concolor*), although in other genera it may be rounded, with the central rays extending out to a point.

The anal fins too are quite variable in appearance, being especially long in some species, running the entire length of the body. It means that the ano-genital opening is actually located just behind the head in these fish, being present just in front of the anal fin as in other fish. Its position here may be beneficial during the spawning process, since in most cases the eggs must be retrieved and transferred to the mouth of the fish, even if subsequently they are carried to a nest. Clearly when released close to the mouth they are easier to catch as they fall.

THE LABYRINTH ORGAN

The gills of fish serve to extract oxygen from water passing over them, and ensure that carbon dioxide can diffuse out from the blood too. The movement of the gill covers ensures the flow of water here is maintained, but in anabantoids, their supplementary respiratory system allows them to breathe air too, although their reliance on their labyrinth organs for this purpose varies among species, reflecting their environment.

The air-breathing process is further facilitated by the longer lower lips of many species. This allows fish to break the surface without having to make their presence here conspicuous, which could serve to attract the attentions of fish-eating birds or other predators.

The labyrinth organs are located close to the gills themselves, although their actual structure varies somewhat, being most convoluted in cases where the organs are most efficient. This is because the convolutions or folds increase the surface area of the organs, allowing for more efficient gaseous exchange. While respiration (the release of energy) is a complex process—even in a fish—gas exchange is not. Just as in the gills, the oxygen is transferred simply by moving from a higher concentration in air, to the lower concentration in the blood. This diffusion process occurs in reverse as well, removing carbon dioxide.

Anabantoids do not hatch with functioning labyrinth organs, and so at first they rely entirely on their gills for their respiratory requirements. The transition in life normally commences when the young fish are about three weeks old (*see* page 98), but if kept artificially in a tank with no access to atmospheric oxygen, this stage in their development does not occur. Should the fish subsequently be allowed to breathe air, then they still develop labyrinth organs,

❸ The shape of the fins can be significant in distinguishing the sexes of many anabantoids. In particular, the caudal fins of males are more elaborate than those of females, as in the black paradisefish (*Macropodus concolor*) shown here. The same also applies with the dorsal fin.

although the procedure may not be as complete as if this had taken place at an earlier stage in life.

THE SWIM BLADDER AND SOUND

Anabantoids have a much larger swim bladder than most fish, full of air, that occupies much of the upper part of the body, although it does not benefit from protection by the rib cage as in other groups of fish. This structure aids not only buoyancy and gaseous exchange, but is also vital, in association with the labyrinth organ itself, as a means of amplifying sounds. Living close to the surface, often in relatively shallow waters, anabantoids benefit from being able to detect sounds. This sensory awareness may help them either to find potential prey or avoid predators.

An ability to detect sounds also affords the possibility for these fish to communicate with each other. Unfortunately, the low frequency noise is inaudible to us in most cases, with the exception of the sounds made by the croaking gourami (*Trichopsis vittatus*). The ability to communicate in this way may allow these fish to stay in touch with each other in murky waters, and is also involved in the courtship process, with the sounds being uttered more frequently by both sexes at spawning time.

➊ The calls of the croaking gourami (*Trichopsis vittatus*) help them to find mates, especially in stretches of water where visibility is poor.

THE LATERAL LINE

Further sensory input comes from the lateral line, which runs down each side of the body, in the midline, extending toward the tail. In most but not all cases, this is undivided and is often visible as a pale streak. The lateral line is comprised of a series of nerve cells, connecting directly to the brain. It registers changes in pressure in the water, alerting the fish not only to possible danger, but also to the direction and strength of water currents around them. Such information may be particularly significant to labyrinth fish, helping nest-building males to determine the best area to

construct their nests, minimizing the likelihood of them being broken up and swept away.

LOCOMOTION

The structure of the fins themselves is quite variable, with a significant difference in the number of hard spines that are present. In some anabantoids, the presence of the bony rays in the fins, notably the pelvic fins, has a functional significance. These projections help the fish to move on land. The climbing perch (*Anabas testudineus*), which is actually an anabantoid in spite of its name, is capable of moving as far as 600ft (180m) over the course of a night, using its pelvic fins as well as the spines on its gill covers to provide it with locomotive traction. Only short trips overland are usually necessary, allowing the fish to track back to deeper waters as the floodplains start to dry out after the end of the rainy season. The presence of spines can also be a deterrent to predators encountering these fish out of water. In some cases, these fins can also assist the fish to bury themselves in the muddy base of their pools, before these dry out completely. Here, like lungfish, they may remain entombed and alive, awaiting the rains that will restore their aquatic habitat.

The pelvic fins are located in a forward position, just behind the gills and have a prominent hard ray. They have also been modified into sensory appendages, being long and narrow in shape in *Trichogaster* and *Colisa* species. In these anabantoids, they serve as organs of taste as well as touch, with their length and forward positioning being useful for these purposes.

⦿ The lateral line runs down each side of a fish's body, roughly in the position where the lighter horizontal markings are evident in these Vaillant's chocolate gouramis (*Sphaerichthys vaillantii*). It provides the fish with vital sensory information.

STOCKING DENSITIES

While some anabantoids are highly territorial, others instinctively school together as a defense against predators, especially while they are young. The coloration of many gouramis affords them further protection, breaking up their shape with a range of stripes so that predators find it harder to target an individual in a school, or spot one of these fish lurking in among aquatic vegetation.

In the wild, anabantoids can space themselves out, with the natural cover provided by plants helping them to establish territories and boundaries. This is not possible within the confines of an aquarium, which is why it is important not to overcrowd the fish in these surroundings. The level of aggression is likely to increase as young male anabantoids mature, and as they come into breeding condition. Even if there is no direct physical conflict, the constant harrying is likely to cause stress, leaving the weaker individual more vulnerable to opportunistic infections.

Anabantoids communicate through a series of warnings to each other before launching into an attack, with the intention of intimidating their would-be rival. In croaking gouramis (*Trichopsis* spp.), the dominant call of a male may be sufficient to deter conflict by intimidating a weaker individual. Visual signs are also important, with male Siamese fighting fish (*Betta splendens*) seeking to flare their gill covers and extend their fins. This has the effect of making them appear larger, but if this does not cause a rival to back away, then they will swim in close proximity to each other, moving their fins to create currents. These register via the lateral line, and are another indicator of the fish's strength. If the conflict continues, the anabantoids will then come into direct physical contact, starting to beat each other with their fins.

⊘ REFLECTION REFLEX

Male Siamese fighting fish (*Betta splendens* (*right*)) will respond aggressively to reflected images of themselves in mirrors, so be sure not to place a mirror in close proximity to their aquarium. Otherwise, the male is likely to become stressed or injured by constantly challenging and seeking to attack his own reflection.

Fighting is most likely to occur not with one male much larger than a rival, but in cases where the fish are evenly matched. The final warning is indicated by the combatants seeking to bite each other's caudal fin. Should neither give way at this point, then serious conflict is inevitable. The fish launch into a direct frontal assault, usually grabbing each other's jaws, and wrestling ferociously. This physical exertion demands a lot of energy, with the result that at intervals the fish are likely to break away from each other and swim to the surface, in order to obtain more oxygen to sustain their challenge. Conflict then resumes, and can last for over an hour, as the fish tussle violently.

The fight may end suddenly, with the weaker individual abandoning its challenge by clamping its fins down and raising its head in the water, to indicate its submission, before escaping from the area. Once the loser is out of the other fish's territory, it will not be pursued. This is where problems arise in the aquarium, because there is insufficient space for an individual to escape, resulting in the weaker individual being badly mauled and even killed. There is also a significant risk of aggression if a female is introduced at the wrong time to a would-be mate.

🔵 Some gouramis, such as the pearl (*Trichogaster leeri*) and spotted (*T. trichopterus*), are social, but keeping different yet closely related species together may result in unwanted hybridization if the fish breed.

CHOOSING AN AQUARIUM

It is important to decide from the outset whether you want to keep one group of anabantoids together, or incorporate some of these fish in a community aquarium alongside other types of fish. The commonly available species are quite adaptable in their water chemistry requirements, and can be maintained without great difficulty, although certainly for breeding purposes a more specialized setup is required, catering for the individual needs of the particular species chosen.

The approximate adult size of the anabantoids is another consideration in determining their housing, as some of the larger species of course require large aquariums.

Although there are so-called "aquarium kits" these are often rather small to house many anabantoids, and their design may be unsuitable for these fish, as there should be a gap for air above the water. This may not be possible where the heater extends in a vertical casing right to the roof of the aquarium. They can be useful for smaller members of the genus, as they have a stylish design which hides much of the hardware, as well as being simple to set up.

These complete units are made from acrylic, which is relatively lightweight, but tanks made from this material can be scratched more easily than those made of glass. The advent of silicone rubber sealant for aquarium use has meant that glass aquariums can be constructed in virtually any size or shape, with the thickness of glass required and buttressing, in the form of supporting bars at the top of the tank, depending on its size. Triangular designs which can be fitted into the corner of a room are one possibility, although bear in mind that if you opt for one of these less traditional designs you will also need a corresponding aquarium hood.

POSITIONING THE AQUARIUM

Since a gallon of water weighs the equivalent of 8lb (3.6kg), it is vital to choose the correct site in the room for the aquarium at the outset. Otherwise, you have to catch the fish, strip down the tank and empty it before relocating it elsewhere, simply because it is too heavy to move when full. Practical considerations such as proximity to an electical outlet are important, to avoid the necessity of trailing wires around the room. Sitting down can help when deciding the best location, as this allows you to check where you are likely to get the best view of the aquarium and its occupants. Avoid locations next to televisions and stereos because the sound vibrations may disturb the fish in the water.

The weight of water within the aquarium means that it must be adequately supported on a secure base. An existing piece of furniture in the room may be suitable for this purpose, but alternatively there are metal stands and even cabinets, made in various styles and of different wood finishes, which are suitable for this purpose. It is usual to rest silicone glass tanks directly on a bed of styrofoam that extends to support all four corners, to absorb any unevenness in the

---

ⓘ HEAT IN THE HOME

Choose an area out of direct sunlight, since on a hot day, this can cause the water temperature to rise to a fatal level for gouramis remarkably quickly. Furthermore, this bright light is liable to cause excessive algal growth in the tank, turning the sides green. Equally, avoid potentially drafty locations, such as halls, especially if you are setting up a breeding tank, because the cold air can have devastating effects on the young anabantoids while their labyrinth organs are developing. It is also a bad idea to sit the tank next to a radiator, for obvious reasons.

surface beneath. If your floor slopes significantly, then it is worthwhile correcting any imbalance here when pulling the tank in
place. Check its positioning with a spirit level at this stage, before
filling it.

CLEANLINESS

Although the tank may be new, it is still worth wiping it out first
before filling it, as it could easily be dusty. Running some water into
the base also enables you to check that it does not leak, although
a visual check to ensure the sealant is evenly distributed around the
inside of the tank should alert you to any problem in this regard. If
you have acquired a second-hand tank, then stand it outdoors on
a piece of styrofoam and fill it with a solution of aquarium disinfectant, in order to kill off any potentially harmful microbes, before
washing it out thoroughly.

Aquarium gravel, even that which is sold as prewashed, is likely
to benefit from being washed again before being placed in the
aquarium. This can be carried out easily using a colander.

THE AQUARIUM FLOOR

The undergravel filter plate itself needs to be put in place first,
covering the entire base of the aquarium, before the gravel is added.
The gravel needs to be relatively coarse—this is especially important
when incorporating an undergravel filter, which is frequently used

There are different
colors of gravel
available, aside from
the natural variety.
White gravel can be
attractive with certain
species, such as pearl
gouramis (*Trichogaster
leeri*), as it serves to
highlight their
markings.

with anabantoids, as the water needs to pass easily between the particles of gravel.

There are various types of gravel on the market today, some of which are brightly colored, but these often detract from the actual appearance of the fish, draining color from them. There are some exceptions, but you need to be cautious in this regard—kissing gouramis (*Helostoma temminckii*) show to good effect against a blackish substrate, but red gravel drains the color from many bettas. It is also worth bearing in mind that not only can these fish see in color, so that this type of base covering could be disorientating to them, but also that they tend to inhabit areas where the floor covering is naturally quite dark.

You need to allow about 2.2 pounds (1kg) of gravel per 1.2 gallons (4.5 liters) of tank volume to ensure an adequate base covering in the aquarium.

PLANTING

The choice of plants is especially significant for many anabantoids, because they provide cover and also serve as anchorage points, sometimes being directly incorporated into the bubblenests. Although living plants are harder to maintain, they are a better option when breeding bubblenesting species, compared with what may be realistic looking plastic counterparts.

Aquarium plants can be divided into various categories, and a selection of both planted and floating vegetation is usually recommended. Since most anabantoids are quite adaptable in their water chemistry requirements, a range of plants can be used in their aquarium. Greater care has to be taken when selecting plants that can grow under brackish water conditions, but this is not of great concern with the vast majority of anabantoids.

You can simply purchase a selection of plants, as recommended for the size of the aquarium. Nevertheless, it is important to have a planting scheme in

➊ When planning the layout of the tank, it is important to leave open space so the fish can swim without difficulty. Rockwork needs to be securely positioned within the aquarium, while the air uplift connecting to the undergravel filter can be disguised by taller plants.

mind so that the plants can be incorporated effectively into the overall design of the aquarium. Many aquarium plants come in the form of cuttings, with few roots. Even so, it may be a good idea to set these in smaller flat containers that can be concealed with gravel, simply because otherwise their roots may ultimately grow down and block off the slits in the undergravel filter, reducing its efficiency accordingly.

Surface cover

The banana plant (*Nymphoides aquatica*) is a good choice for a plant that provides cover over the surface of the water. Related to water lilies, it has a similar pattern of growth, even occasionally flowering above the water surface, and has an unusual appearance below the water level too, thanks to its bananalike roots. Its disklike leaves, which float at the surface, may be supported on stems up to 12in (30cm) long, making it ideal for the average anabantoid aquarium.

A similar but larger plant, of African rather than American origin, is the African tiger lotus (*Nymphaea maculata*). This is often sold in the form of rhizomes, which simply need to be potted up, and should start to grow readily. There are special aquatic plant fertilizers available if you want to give the vegetation in the tank a boost, but burying a few rabbit droppings around the roots can be just as effective.

Buying rhizomes has the added advantage that the leaves do not die back after being moved. Always ensure that aquatic plants are kept moist at all times, and transfer them back under water without delay, handling any leaves as little as possible. This should minimize problems, although they take time to establish themselves in new surroundings.

● Good cover over the surface of the water can be provided by the banana plant (*Nymphoides aquatica*), which is a relative of the water lilies.

AQUARIUM SNAILS

There is always a possibility that aquatic snails may turn up unexpectedly in the aquarium, having been introduced on plants. It is not always easy to spot their transparent, jelly-like eggs on the back of the leaves. In small numbers, snails can be beneficial, eating remnants of food while providing an additional source of interest in the aquarium, but they can easily build up to reach plague proportions, stripping the leaves of the plants. This is because they are hermaphrodite, and so every individual is capable of producing hundreds of fertile eggs. Luckily, some gouramis help keep the numbers of these invertebrates in check naturally, by feeding on them. In other cases, if you need to catch the snails to remove them, prop an upturned saucer up on the floor of the aquarium, and place a piece of cucumber here. When you lift out the saucer in the morning, you should find a number of snails have tracked it down to congregate underneath.

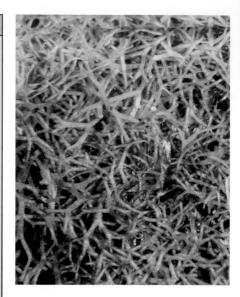

Never bury the crowns of aquatic plants or rhizomes when planting them. This is important, because otherwise, they will simply rot away. Similarly, with cuttings, strip off the lower two pairs of leaves, to prevent them dying away, and encourage the development of new roots.

Floating plants are easy to establish, with many such as Amazon frogbit (*Limnobium laevigatum*) spreading rapidly over the surface, to the extent that their growth may need to be curtailed. One of the best floating plants for anabantoids is *Riccia fluitans*, as this plant is ideal in providing anchorage sites for bubblenests. With a gap present between the water surface and the aquarium hood, slightly taller floating plants can also be added, such as water lettuce (*Pistia stratiotes*).

DECOR WITHIN THE TANK

Although plants help to provide cover, it is important to provide other retreats, particularly for the ornate gourami or malpulutta (*Malpulutta kretseri*), which spawns in caves. Molded lightweight designs of caves and rocks are available in aquatic stores, while rockwork can also be carefully incorporated, taking care to ensure that it cannot be dislodged. It is vital not to use limestone rocks, since these slowly dissolve over a period of time, altering the water chemistry, causing the water to become harder. Most stores stock a range of suitable pieces of rock, sold by weight. All rockwork to be used in the aquarium should be scrubbed using an aquarium disinfectant, and then rinsed thoroughly.

Plants can also be grown on rocks, softening their outline. Typical examples that are easily grown in this way are Java fern (*Microsorum pteropus*) and Java moss (*Vesicularia dubyana*), being held in place initially by a rubber band until they anchor themselves on to the rocks. Java moss particularly is well suited to growing in the depths of the aquarium where the light level is low.

Riccia fluitans is an ideal floating plant for anabantoids, providing excellent anchorage sites for bubblenests.

Growing aquatic plants on and among the rockwork creates a naturalistic impression in the tank. Common sense dictates tall plants are at the back.

Bogwood can be included in an aquarium for anabantoids, and again, you are likely to find some interesting shapes for sale at most outlets catering for aquarium hobbyists. The wood itself should be soaked for a period in a bucket of water with the water changed daily, because otherwise the tannins in the wood are likely to leach out into the tank water, turning it yellow. Some fish keepers paint bogwood with varnish, to seal it, but there is a slight risk that if any of the fish in the aquarium nibble at the varnish coating, then they may poison themselves.

POWERED EQUIPMENT

Heating

The development of reliable heaters has done much to facilitate the keeping of anabantoids, since the water temperature in their aquaria can now be maintained easily. The development of heaters has also meant that there is no need to have a separate thermostat to control the output from the heater, as a thermostat is incorporated into the unit. Most are preset to approximately 77°F (25°C), but they can normally be adjusted without difficulty as required. Heaters are available in various lengths, and for anabantoids, where the water level may be relatively low, a fairly short unit is preferable. As a guide, allow about 8 watts per gallon (3.8liters), based on the tank's volume.

The water temperature itself is monitored easily by means of an external digital thermostat, stuck on the outside of the glass where it can be read at a glance. There are normally no problems with heaters, but if you do purchase a secondhand aquarium it is worthwhile to replace the heater, since they do have a limited lifespan, maybe lasting three years on average. You can then be sure that the unit does not fail soon afterward in your new set-up.

> ⓘ **HEATER ADJUSTMENT**
>
> **When altering the temperature on a heater, ensure that the electricity is turned off before you remove the unit from the aquarium. Make sure the unit is positioned correctly in the water before the electricity is turned back on.**

A

B

C

❶ A range of aquarium equipment.
A. Heaters incorporating a thermostat are available in different sizes.
B. An external thermostat with a temperature probe.
C. A liquid crystal display (LCD) thermometer. Simpler designs, which can be stuck to the side of the aquarium, are also available.

Lighting

Aquarium lighting has also advanced significantly over recent years. Its purpose should be not only to make the fish more visible, but also to provide the essential light energy to allow the plants to photosynthesize and create energy, helping to ensure healthy growth. When they are photosynthesizing, the plants also release oxygen into the water, which can benefit the fish.

Fluorescent tubes sold for this purpose emit light of specific wavelengths corresponding closely to those of sunlight, and minimal heat compared with incandescent bulbs, which are unsuitable for this reason. The tubes are produced in various lengths, corresponding to that of aquarium hoods. They need to be kept well away from water, and so are effectively sealed into the hood.

The lights should be left on for approximately 8–10 hours every day, although if you find that the tank is suffering from a build-up of bright green algae, it is worthwhile cutting back on the length of time that the lights are on. Anabantoids generally prefer fairly subdued lighting, and the presence of floating plants in the aquarium helps to replicate such conditions.

Nocturnal fluorescent lights are a quite recent development, which enable you to watch your fish's behavior after dark. This can be particularly valuable in a community

aquarium, when some fish often become more active at this time, being far less entertaining during the daytime.

FILTRATION

An undergravel filter affords a relatively gentle method of filtration, compared with a power filter. These units incorporate their own pump, and are sold in different sizes for various tank volumes. The outlet at the top of the filter is kept just above the surface of the water. The resulting current not only serves to improve the oxygenation of the water but, perhaps more significantly, especially in a well-planted tank, also helps to ensure that the temperature of the water in the aquarium is fairly even, with no localized hot or cold spots.

The undergravel filter plate serves as the filter bed, in which a beneficial population of bacteria will soon become established, serving to break down the waste produced by the fish. This is really a microcosm of what happens in the natural environment. The bacteria convert the relative toxic ammonia to less damaging nitrite and then to nitrate, which can in turn be utilized by the plants as a fertilizer.

In a new aquarium, it is possible to speed up the development of the filter bed by adding a starter culture of these bacteria, which multiply rapidly in the presence of oxygen. This is why it is necessary to operate an air pump as part of the filter system, and keep it running constantly—it is important to choose the quietest design of air pump you can find. Under no circumstances should the air pump be covered to muffle the noise, because this is likely to constitute a fire hazard To be safe, it should also be fitted with a one way valve, so there is no risk of water from the tank being drawn back into the unit.

A power filter may be divided into various chambers, within its plastic casing. There is likely to be a filter sponge here at the very least. This serves both as a mechanical and a biological filter, removing and trapping particulate matter from the water, while allowing a buildup of beneficial bacteria in the foam, which in turn supplements the work of the undergravel filter in dealing with nitrogenous waste matter. There may be a carbon core in the power filter cartridge as well, which serves to adsorb chemicals from solution.

Filter maintenance

The danger of the undergravel filter becoming blocked with debris drawn down through the gravel is avoided by using a gravel cleaner. Take care not to uproot growing plants. With a power filter, the cartridge at the core needs washing out at intervals, because it becomes blocked, which potentially reduces the flow rate significantly.

Never be tempted to wash the foam out under a running faucet in a sink, because, apart from concerns about hygiene, this has detrimental effects on the functioning of the filter. The chlorine or chloramine in the water destroys the beneficial bacteria that are integral to the filtration process. Only wash the filter core out in a bucket of water that has been previously siphoned out of the aquarium, as this water is safe to use for this purpose. The water should then be discarded down an outside drain, or tipped over a flowerbed, with the bonus of the nitrate it contains acting as a plant fertilizer.

On occasions, it is necessary to replace the filter cartridge. When you do, add a bacterial culture to start the filter off again. More frequent water changes are usually advisable for several weeks afterwards.

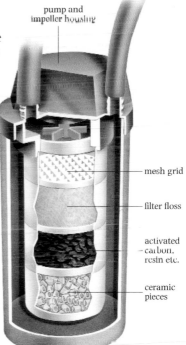

pump and impeller housing

mesh grid

filter floss

activated carbon, resin etc.

ceramic pieces

● A typical power filter comprises several chambers, which may incorporate different methods of filtration.

! STRENGTH OF CURRENT

Although power filters can be beneficial for routine use in aquariums housing anabantoids, they are not generally suitable for breeding set-ups, because the currents they produce at the water surface destroy bubblenests. Once the fry hatch, they are likely to be drawn into the unit and become trapped. A simple sponge filter is recommended for this type of set-up.

WATER CHEMISTRY

There are two significant aspects to water chemistry, as far as keeping fish is concerned: the relative acidity of the water (or pH), and its degree of hardness (or softness) often measured on the dGH scale. There are various test kits available that can give you a clear reading, not to mention more sophisticated LCD metering devices. As far as pH is concerned, this is measured using a logarithmic scale extending from 0 up to 14, with figures up to 7.0 being regarded as acidic water conditions, while those above this neutral figure are alkaline. Owing to the scale used, even a small shift in the pH reading has a significant environmental impact. Anabantoids are generally found in the wild in waters which are slightly acidic, partly as a result of the presence of often dense aquatic vegetation.

There is no single equivalent to the pH scale for assessing the relative hardness of water. Instead, there are a number of different measuring systems. Even so, just washing your hands or looking at the inside of your kettle will reveal whether the water in your area is hard or soft. It is difficult to create a lather with soap in hard water areas, and there will be an evident build-up of white deposits on the inside of a kettle.

This is the result of the precipitation of calcium and magnesium bicarbonate salts, which are responsible for what is known as temporary hardness, and can be deposited out of solution by boiling. Permanent hardness is caused by sulfates of calcium and magnesium, as well as other chemicals such as nitrates.

The source of the water has a marked effect on whether it is hard or soft. Rainwater is soft. In contrast, water that has run over or filtered down through limestone beds is hard, having acquired

bicarbonate salts during this period. It is quite easy to increase the hardness when required in soft-water areas, simply by adding calcium in the form of rockwork or as gravel that gradually dissolves into the water. This also has the effect of making the water more alkaline.

◑ Chocolate gourami country, Malaysia; many anabantoids are found in areas of dense aquatic veget- ation, which makes for acidic water.

Conversely, water softening can be carried out by adding a suitable volume of fresh rainwater to the existing supply, although in reality, with fears over the presence of pollutants in rainwater, most fish keepers prefer to use a device called a hydrogen deionizer for this purpose. As the name suggests, this unit basically switches hydrogen ions for calcium ones, but does not affect the pH. When a more acid pH is required, this is normally achieved by adding a packet of aquarium peat to the power filter. It needs to be changed about once every three weeks to remain active.

WATER CHANGES

The most important thing for keeping the anabantoids in good health is to carry out regular partial water changes. A special siphon system is useful for this task, serving also as a gravel cleaner to ensure that the undergravel filter continues to work at maximum efficiency. This attachment to the tube agitates the gravel as it sucks up water, taking dirt with it.

WATER SAFETY

Fresh water straight from the faucet is potentially dangerous to anabantoids and other fish, since it contains chlorine or chloramine, which is a combination of chlorine and ammonia. While chlorine dissipates from water left to stand for about 24 hours, chloramine is a much more stable compound that can remain hazardous to fish for a week, unless it is neutralized. Water conditioners, which fulfill this task, should be added in the requisite volume to the water, before it is poured into the aquarium. These products also contain other beneficial ingredients, such as aloe vera, which helps to protect the fish from infection.

The frequency of water changes depends partly on the length of time that the tank has been set up, as well as the stocking density, since more frequent water changes are needed in new tanks, where the filtration system takes about two months to start working at maximum efficiency.

⬆ The growing requirements of plants must be met if they are to thrive. Java moss (*Vesicularia dubyana*) is one of the most adaptable species, which thrives even in brackish water.

This is because it takes time for the necessary build-up of the beneficial bacteria to take place. During this time, water quality problems can arise, creating deaths from what is often described as "New Tank Syndrome," unless water quality is strictly monitored—test kits are available for this purpose and should be used. The addition of packets of zeolite, which removes ammonia produced by the fish, can be especially useful at this stage, by lessening the burden on the filtration system.

In rearing tanks too, when the level of filtration is relatively low and the stocking density often quite high, frequent partial water changes are vital to the well-being of the fry, and are required every two or three days. What is equally important, especially for young fish, is that the water that is replaced is at the same temperature as that within the tank itself. This can be achieved by using a spare heater to warm the water in a bucket overnight, not forgetting to add a water conditioner as well.

BRACKISH SURROUNDINGS

Under normal circumstances, it is usually not necessary to keep anabantoids in brackish water, although a few species, such as the climbing perch (*Anabas testudineus*) can be found in such surroundings in the wild. If necessary, a special marine salt mix can be obtained to create a suitable brackish environment. This needs to be stirred into the tank water to ensure that it is properly dissolved, creating a weaker strength solution than that used in marine tanks. The amount of marine salt required to create the required brackish set-up is indicated on the pack, relative to the volume of the tank.

As far as plants are concerned, only some of the hardier species grow well in brackish water. Nevertheless, both Java moss (*Vesicularia dubyana*) and Java fern (*Microsorum pteropus*) thrive in these surroundings, as do other plants that are often grown in aquaria accommodating anabantoids, including hornwort (*Ceratophyllum*) as well as eel grass (*Vallisneria spiralis*).

Whenever carrying out a partial water change, you need to add the requisite amount of marine salt, but if the water evaporates, bear in mind that the salt level will have risen in the remaining volume of water, and dechlorinated fresh water will be required to dilute it again. The salt level in water is measured on the specific gravity (SG) scale using a hygrometer—freshwater gives an SG reading of 1.000, with brackish water reading up to approximately 1.010,

FILLING THE TANK

Once you have prepared the base and put the heater in place, you can then start to add the water to the aquarium. A clean plastic watercan is useful for this purpose, especially since most watercans have a stated volume, allowing you to add the correct volume of water conditioner before pouring the water into the tank. If you place a saucer of some kind on the gravel, this helps to dissipate the force of the water, preventing the gravel base from being disturbed.

Once the tank is about half-full, you can then set the plants in the gravel, based on the planting scheme devised earlier. Putting them into position at this stage reduces the likelihood of them being uprooted as you continue to fill the tank. Finally, once it is relatively full, leave a gap at the top of the water to accommodate the floating plants, which can be added last.

With dry hands, plug in the various electrical components such as the heater and a power filter. Check that the equipment is all working properly, carrying out any minor adjustments before adding the fish once the water temperature has stabilized. It is better to set up the aquarium several days beforehand, to ensure everything is functioning correctly and that the plants are firmly set in place.

With the stocking level being crucial to the well-being of the anabantoids, it is important that they are not overcrowded at any stage. When purchasing young fish, always allow for their likely adult size, and do not overlook their potentially pugnacious nature either, which is likely to become more apparent as they mature.

◐ A few anabantoids are found in brackish environments, notably the climbing perch (*Anabas testudineus*).

CHAPTER 4

Feeding Habits and Food

The naturally adaptable feeding habits of anabantoids has meant that feeding them in the aquarium is generally quite straightforward, especially as there are foods available that have been devised to mirror their feeding instincts. The widespread availability of not just prepared foods but also suitable live foods has facilitated the successful breeding of these fish, and this has also helped to increase their popularity.

⬇ Anything for a free meal; a pearl gourami (*Trichogaster leeri*) foraging for catfish pellets on the base of the aquarium. Usually gouramis seek food closer to the surface, but most are quite adaptable.

MOUTH FACTORS

The undershot lower jaw that is clearly apparent in most anabantoids gives a significant insight into the way they feed. These are fish that are not well equipped to search for food on the floor of the aquarium, but in the upper reaches of the water. They can seize insects or other edible items on the surface, or catch food that is floating through the water.

The mouth of most anabantoids is relatively small compared with their body size, and this restricts the size of the food particles they can consume. Those with the widest gape, such as the

Sandelia species, are more predatory by nature, being able to hunt other fish, although other anabantoids feed occasionally on their own fry.

Most species are omnivorous, being aided by the presence of teeth in their mouth and others farther back in the pharyngeal region of the throat. The kissing gourami (*Helostoma temminckii*) is an exception, as its teeth are located on its thick fleshy lips. Enlarged lips of this type are associated with other members of the group, such as the thick-lipped gourami (*Colisa labiosa*), and indicate a diet based in part on algae. This plant growth needs to be rasped off the rocks, with the lips providing an anchorage point, making it easier for the teeth to be used. The constant friction with the rock surfaces may actually enhance the development of the lips, enabling them to function more effectively.

The kissing gourami also has another way of obtaining food, which is especially useful in shallow, warm waters where microscopic plankton thrive. These fish are able to filter the tiny organisms out from the water, using their gill rakers for this purpose, and although it may not be possible to replicate these feeding conditions in the aquarium, plankton-based foods are available. Even so, in common with other anabantoids, aside from the predatory pikehead (*Luciocephalus* spp.), kissing gouramis are quite adaptable in their feeding requirements.

The undershot lower jaw is a typical adaptation seen in fish such as gouramis that feed at the surface.

HUNTING TECHNIQUES

Since many anabantoids occur in fairly shallow waters, it is perhaps not surprising that their sense of sight helps these fish to locate their food. This is especially significant with anabantoids that seek live quarry, whether in the water or above it. Pikeheads (*Luciocephalus* spp.) swim quickly at their prey once it is within reach, hoping to grab their target before it appreciates the danger. Good eyesight is obviously helpful in determining the correct moment to launch into a strike.

One genus of gourami has evolved a particularly sophisticated way of hunting down invertebrates that are out of the water. *Colisa* gouramis have the ability to shoot a jet of water out of their mouth, with the aim of causing their prey to fall into the water where it can be snapped up. This is a similar but less refined technique to that adopted by the archerfish (*Toxotes* spp.) of South America, that can fire a jet of water up to 3ft (1m), to knock down an insect in flight or one which is resting on overhanging vegetation, catching it unawares so that it falls into the water. Although both groups of fish use an identical mechanism to propel the water forcibly from their mouths, by thrusting out their gill covers, archerfish have an additional refinement, with their palate and tongue combining to form a tube that provides greater propulsive thrust. *Colisa* gouramis are not able to produce such a powerful jet of water, and their range is more restricted as a result.

◑ The differences seen in the patterning of the orange bushfish (*Ctenopoma ansorgii*) may help to disguise its presence in different types of habitat, allowing it to catch prey more easily.

Colisa gouramis can locate potential food by means other than sight, however, thanks to the long, threadlike nature of their pectoral fins. This is a feature they share with members of the *Trichogaster* genus, although it is believed that these sensory structures are probably more significant for interactions between the fish themselves, rather than for finding food. They may use these fins for detecting the presence of small water creatures that they hunt, especially in areas where the water is murky.

African labyrinth fish are generally more predatory in their feeding habits than their Asian relatives, and prefer to hunt at night in some cases. Their jaws are modified, allowing them to seize other fish as well as invertebrates. There are differences in feeding within the bushfish grouping, which tend to reflect the size of the species concerned.

⬇ Banded patterning, as displayed by the banded ctenopoma (C. *fasciolatum*), breaks up the fish's shape so that it can both hunt and hide more effectively.

Smaller bushfish such as the orange bushfish (*Ctenopoma ansorgii*), which grows to a maximum of about 3in (7.5cm), are far less piscivorous by nature than their bigger relatives, preferring to feed instead on invertebrates. In the aquarium, they may even eat some vegetable matter, as does the banded ctenopoma (*C. fasciolatum*), which is one of the more widely kept species.

In Asia, the climbing perches (*Anabas* spp.) rank as true omnivores, quite capable of eating smaller fish. The only truly predatory species among the Asiatic anabantoids are the pikeheads, belonging to the genus *Luciocephalus*. These are ambush predators, seizing fish and invertebrates that pass within their reach, and they are unusual in having keen hearing for this purpose.

The pikehead's labyrinth organs serve predominantly as sound detectors, connecting to the inner ear, rather than being used primarily for auxiliary breathing. Sound waves travel slowly though water, and this mechanism helps pikeheads to detect possible prey when lurking in among aquatic vegetation, with their visibility obscured and their lateral line system blocked off to an extent by their surroundings.

FARM FEEDING

The ease with which most of the larger gouramis can be fed makes them easy to breed commercially, as they are in large numbers in Asia. Few species are more adaptable in this respect than the largest member of the group, the giant gourami (*Osphronemus goramy*), which is often referred to through the region as the "water pig." This is not only because of its appetite, but also because of the way in which these fish are frequently housed in stock ponds.

They are often fed on little more than a diet of pig manure, being housed directly beneath the slatted floor where the pigs are kept, so their waste falls into the water. The relatively inefficient digestive system of the pigs leaves a significant proportion of undigested vegetable matter for the fish to eat, and when provided with this food, the gouramis reach a saleable size within three years.

Kissing gouramis (*Helostoma temminckii*) are often reared in a similar fashion, and both for the adults and the young fish there is

◉ Kissing gouramis (*Helostoma temminckii*) feed on plant matter to a significant extent, and may help to curb the build-up of algae within the aquarium. This pair are displaying the typical kissing posture, which actually represents a test of strength between them.

a further benefit in this type of diet—the high level of organic matter in solution, combined with the warmth ensures that microscopic plankton multiply rapidly in the water, offering an additional source of nutrients, along with insects that are attracted to lay their eggs in the water.

Gouramis benefit from living in shallow pools, because it is here, under the influence of sunlight, that algal growth also flourishes, a significant component in the diet of various species such as the kissing gourami.

Lurking within the algae are tiny microscopic creatures that are also consumed, albeit often inadvertently by the fish when they are browsing on these mats of vegetation. Thus although they may appear to be eating a diet based mainly on plant matter, they are receiving the benefits associated with animal protein as well.

In aquarium surroundings, where algal growth is generally discouraged, these gouramis may turn their attention to plants, and giant gouramis in particular may inflict serious damage, especially if alternative sources of vegetable food are not provided. Although manufactured diets are ideal in their nutritional content, they are relatively concentrated rations, tending to be low in fiber. So bulking up the gourami's rations in this way can be beneficial. The nutritional content of vegetable matter is low, meaning that fish need to consume relatively large amounts in order to meet their nutritional needs.

⊕ Insects such as mosquito larvae (*Culex* sp.) help to supplement the protein intake of anabantoids, and can prove to be a useful breeding conditioner for aquarium fish.

A BASIC DIET

Anabantoids require the same basic nutrients as ourselves, despite the constituents of their diet being significantly different. Their growth depends on proteins, and specifically the amino acids that make up the protein chains themselves. Some of these amino acids are described as "essential," which means that they must be present in the fish's diet if it is not to suffer a nutritional deficiency.

Protein from plants is more likely to be deficient in these key amino acids than is protein of animal origin, which is why items such as insect larvae are important in the diets of these fish. Aside from being vital for growth in young fish, these foods also help to trigger spawning behavior in older individuals.

The levels of carbohydrate and fat in the diet of these fish are critical to their well-being. Carbohydrate is used to provide a readily accessible source of energy in the body, although excessive amounts result in carbohydrate being converted to fat, and stored in the body. The metabolism of young anabantoids may allow them to utilize fat more efficiently, but it can still have potentially harmful consequences, worse in older individuals. Their bodies are generally not well equipped to cope with this dietary component, and foods offered to them should therefore contain less than 8 percent fat as a guide, to mirror their natural diets where fat does not feature prominently. Just as with proteins, however, there are certain components found in fats, known as essential fatty acids, which are vital, especially for the growth of young anabantoids.

MICRONUTRIENTS

Other key ingredients—vitamins, minerals, and trace elements—must also be present in the diets of labyrinth fish, although only in small quantities. These may be critical to various biochemical reactions taking place in the body, as with members of the Vitamin B group, or for the actual growth of the fish, as with calcium, which is vital both for the structure of the skeleton and the functioning of the nervous system.

Such items are usually present in the fish's diet, and in prepared foods are often supplemented accordingly. The addition of stabilized Vitamin C to such foods is a relatively recent development, but manufacturers claim that this enhances the fish's ability to fight infections, thus helping to prevent illness.

The vitamin content is only be maintained for a period, however, depending on the storage conditions of the food. Always leave the lid firmly on, to exclude the air as far as possible, and keep the tub in a relatively cool location, and out of direct sunlight. It is particularly important that dry fish food of any type is not allowed to become wet, otherwise it has to be discarded because it rapidly turns moldy and unfit for use.

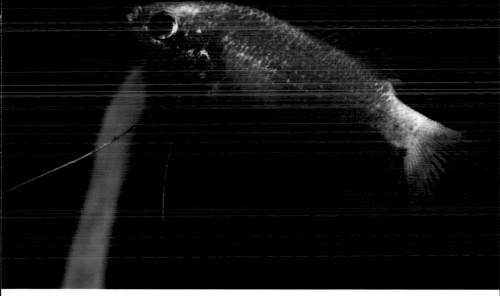

AQUARIUM DIETS

A host of prepared diets is now available for tropical fish, and many of these can be offered to anabantoids. Even so, in the first instance you must match the size of the food particles to the size of the species concerned, especially given the small mouths of many members of this group of fish, and the fact they often prefer to feed at the surface. Anabantoids kept as part of a community aquarium are often fed on a general flake food that is suitable for most fish.

There are now some special diets available for this group of fish, which have been carefully formulated to reflect their dependence on small invertebrates and plant matter. These are typically manufactured from ingredients such as shrimp meal and valued for their unsaturated fatty acid content, along with vegetable matter such as algae and even ground rice. These foods are complete in the sense that they are also supplemented as necessary with vitamins, minerals, and trace elements at the appropriate levels.

Anabantoids fed on such diets should remain in good health, and be well-colored, with their diet influencing their appearance. If keeping Siamese fighting fish (*Betta splendens*), and other species with red coloration, then the use of a specific color food may help to enhance this feature. There is no need to stick to the same food every day—some breeders rely on several suitable diets, alternating them so that the fish receive more variety as a result and benefit accordingly.

⬆ The color of some gouramis can be improved by color-feeding, using either natural agents, such as carrot, or more typically now, special diets produced for this purpose. This is a color-fed *Colisa* sp.

⬆ Paradisefish (*Macropodus opercularis*) with a food pellet. Try to match the size of the fish with the grade of pellets being used as food. This can help to prevent wastage.

The largest members of the group take other floating foods, in the form of food sticks or pellets. Always be cautious when feeding the fish, so as to avoid wastage. Generally, you should aim to offer no more than they will eat within five minutes, feeding them several times during the course of the day. Err on the side of caution at first, until you can be sure of the amount of food that is needed.

OTHER PREPARED FOODS

There are other foods, aside from staple diets, that can be beneficial for anabantoids, although these are not balanced foods in the sense they are unlikely to be supplemented with vitamins or other essential dietary components in most cases. Foods of this type include freeze-dried items such as tubifex worms and krill, which is a zooplankton, containing both microscopic plants and animals. Although of marine origins, it serves to replicate the plankton which these fish naturally eat. Freeze-drying is an effective way of preserving food, by removing water from it. As a result, freeze-dried foods can be kept in ordinary tubs, just like fish food, without the need for refrigeration, and they can be fed straight from the container, floating on the surface at first.

There is a risk with using live foods that they may contain harmful microbes, but this danger is avoided by selecting gamma-irradiated foodstuffs. These need to be kept deep-frozen, and are usually supplied in small packs—it is usually possible to carefully shave off the required amount for the fish with a knife, and allow it to defrost completely, rather than having to thaw out the entire quantity. A wide range of items is available in this form, but mosquito larvae, bloodworm, and daphnia are among those most useful for feeding to anabantoids.

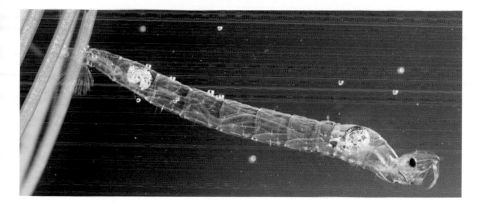

There are also supplementary foods available, including combinations such as tubifex and spirulina algae. Anabantoids, such as kissing gouramis (*Helostoma temminckii*), that naturally feed on algae benefit from this type of food. They can also be offered algal wafers, to supplement their regular diet. These are manufactured using algae combined with vitamins and minerals.

Advances in nutritional technology over recent years have led to the development of foods that combine the palatability and safety of gamma-irradiated foods with the convenience of freeze-dried foods, and do not need to be kept refrigerated. Bloodworm, brine shrimp, and daphnia are all available in this form, and are supplied in packet form.

⊕ The planktonic larvae of the midge *Chaoborus crystallinus*; this particular insect is only found in the wild in ponds without any fish–it somehow knows not to lay its eggs in ponds with fish. So you could say It's an "unnatural" food: the fish don't seem to mind!

GREENSTUFF

There are some anabantoids that consume large quantities of vegetable matter as part of their diet, and it is advisable to supplement their food intake in order to distract their attention away from plants growing in the aquarium. Deep-frozen peas that have been allowed to thaw are popular with larger individuals, as are fresh peas when available. Be sure not to allow uneaten greenstuff to remain in the aquarium, because this will inevitably start to decompose. It can be carefully removed without difficulty in most cases using a net.

LIVE FOODS

It is, of course, possible to provide various invertebrates for anabantoids, and if you are living in a part of the world where these fish

GO ORGANIC

When purchasing greenstuff for anabantoids, it is safer to choose organic products, which should not have any pesticide residues. If you have space in a garden, or even on a window ledge–after all, these fish are Belontiidae, not Balaenidae–grow your own vegetables such as spinach or lettuce. This should guarantee you a fresh supply of leafy food throughout the year.

can be kept in an outdoor pond for at least part of the year, then they will be obtaining some food of this type naturally, along with algae. There are drawbacks in the usage of fresh live foods, especially those of aquatic origins, the biggest risk being that they might introduce diseases to the aquarium occupants.

PREDATORY ANABANTOIDS

If certain anabantoids are kept, notably pikeheads (*Luciocephalus* species), there will be little alternative other than to use live foods. They are far less inclined to take inert foodstuffs, although it may be possible to wean them on to these in due course. With tubifex, the worms have hopefully been cleaned prior to sale, by being kept in clean water. This needs to be changed regularly, and at home they can be stored in a clean jar in a cool place before being offered to the fish.

Special tubifex feeders are available, usually in a cone-shaped design. They can be attached to the side of the aquarium just below the water surface, with the worms protruding through the feeder's small holes, so they can be sucked out by the fish. This is much better than simply tipping a blob of these worms into the aquarium, because they will then burrow into the substrate.

One advantage of tubifex over certain other live foods is that these worms are less likely to die off if uneaten, which could have serious detrimental effects on the water quality. Instead, they are likely to become established in the floor of the aquarium, where the fish may eat them later (if they can get at them). Just as with all inert foodstuffs, it is important to try to match the amount of live food provided to the quantity the fish will eat within a limited period of time.

The risk of disease transmission is highest with aquatic live foods, but there is also the added hazard of introducing other aquatic creatures inadvertently into the aquarium at the same time. This applies especially with daphnia, sometimes known as water fleas because of their jerky swimming motions, although they are actually crustaceans. They are sold in bags of water, and it is important to check by tapping the bag that a significant number remain alive prior to purchase. They should then swim up from the bottom of the bag, becoming more visible in the water.

The easiest and safest way to feed daphnia to the anabantoids is to catch them using a fine strainer and simply rinse them out in the tank. Check closely first for the presence of other creatures that could prey upon any anabantoid fry.

Over the long term, it is useful to set up your own breeding colony of daphnia, which can be done easily if you have a tub of water where there is algal growth. Simply transfer the daphnia here, and before long, they should be breeding. You can catch them in the future with a fine-mesh net, transferring them directly to the aquarium.

This culture is also likely to provide other suitable live foods for the fish as well, particularly in the warmer months of the year, when midges and similar insects are attracted to areas of standing water where they can lay their eggs. The resulting red-colored larvae are known as bloodworms because of their coloration, and they too can be sieved out for the fish, providing a valuable source of nutrients. Mosquito larvae, which form part of the natural diet of many anabantoids, can be collected in a similar way.

The safest forms of live food to offer anabantoids are those which have been specifically cultured for them. Brine shrimp (*Artemia salina*) larvae, known as nauplii, are particularly valuable, not just to supplement the diets of adult fish, but as a rearing food for the fry once they are large enough to eat these crustaceans.

Brine-shrimp eggs can be hatched without great difficulty at home, with commercial kits available for this purpose, or

🔾 Water fleas (daphnia) can be cultured quite easily in a tank outdoors, helping to ensure that there is a constant supply of live food available for your fish.

alternatively, it is simply a matter of setting up a container with salt water, strong aeration and warmth. Vacuum packing ensures that brine-shrimp eggs are most likely to hatch well—they are hygroscopic, attracting moisture from the atmosphere, and this reduces their viability. It is much better to purchase smaller packs as required, rather than a large amount.

Hatching depends on the temperature of the water, taking about 36 hours at 75°F (24°C). It helps to obtain eggs without shells because otherwise, the indigestible shells need to be removed before the larvae can be offered to the fish. It is possible to sieve off the eggshells easily though, since these float at the surface of the water, while the nauplii themselves will be at the bottom of the container. They need to be washed off in dechlorinated water before being offered. Setting up cultures in sequence ensures that you have a constant supply to feed to young gouramis, although it is sometimes possible to obtain live nauplii from aquatic stores.

Although less widely available than brine-shrimp eggs, there are a number of small worms that can also be raised quite easily at home for anabantoids, and microworms can be useful as a food for young fry. These nematodes multiply rapidly, and are obtainable in the first instance from specialist suppliers who advertise in the fish keeping magazines.

Microworms can be reared on a mix of baby cereal food moistened with water, to which a little dried yeast has been added. This should

⬇ Whiteworm (*Enchytraeus albidus*) in a culture. These small worms make a valuable addition to the diet of gouramis.

be kept in a covered container with some small air holes to let the resulting carbon dioxide gas escape. Within a few days, more microworms will soon be evident on the sides of the plastic container. They can be transferred from here directly to the aquarium. Cultures remain productive for up to two weeks, so again, they need to be set up sequentially to guarantee a continuous supply.

Whiteworms (*Enchytraeus*) are larger in size, and in this case, it is likely to take about a month to establish a colony. They are suitable for adult fish, whereas microworms can be fed to anabantoids less than a week old. Bread moistened with milk provides whiteworms with their nourishment, and their container must be kept cool. They should be buried with their food in a moist peat-substitute, and subsequently harvested using tweezers. They can be dropped into a saucer of dechlorinated water to clean them off.

● Bloodworm is a nutritious feeding option for some anabantoids, available in freeze-dried and other forms.

Fruitflies (*Drosophila*) represent another useful food for anabantoids, being easily cultured from a starter kit. They can be reared using a formulated paste, although traditionally they are bred with banana skins serving as their food source. They need to be kept in a jar in a warm location, with the roof of the jar sealed with muslin to prevent any of the flies escaping. Fruitflies have been widely used in genetic studies, and there are actually flightless strains available, which are ideal for use as fish food, as there is no risk of them escaping into the home.

In some areas it may not be possible to use fruitflies, because of the threat they pose to the agricultural industry. There is a useful alternative, however, in the form of hatchling crickets. These are more commonly sold as herptile food, but are taken readily by many anabantoids including pikeheads (*Luciocephalus* spp.), which need a diet based on live food.

Crickets, like other invertebrates, do not offer a balanced diet on their own, as they are deficient in various key constituents, such as calcium. There are special nutritional balancers that can be applied to these insects before they are used as live food, but unfortunately, the benefits are washed away once they are in water, a problem lizard keepers don't have. A different technique, known as gut loading can work under these circumstances, because it relies upon feeding the crickets a diet based on the ingredients that are lacking in their bodies. These are not dissipated by water, remaining within their digestive tracts, and the anabantoids benefit by consuming the entire insect.

USING FRUITFLIES

Tap the side of the jar hard before opening it. This causes the flies to fall to the bottom, and then you can tip a limited number carefully into the water. Always try to avoid any area where there is a dense covering of floating plants at the surface, so that the flies are not out of reach of the fish.

CHAPTER 5

Reproduction

Many anabantoids can be spawned quite easily in the home aquarium, and they display a fascinating range of breeding behavior patterns depending on the species concerned, although all reproduce by laying eggs that are externally fertilized.

PLANNING AHEAD

It is not usually possible to breed these fish successfully in the company of other fish, so they require a special breeding tank for this purpose. A few, such as the chocolate gourami (*Sphaerichthys osphromenoides*), do have a reputation for being more difficult, but success can frequently be achieved even in these cases provided that close attention is paid to the water chemistry.

ⓓ Some gouramis, such as the chocolate gourami (*Sphaerichthys osphromenoides*), have gained a reputation for being harder to breed than others, but this should not in itself be a deterrent to keeping them.

While it may be possible to maintain fish outside the ideal parameters, they are unlikely to spawn successfully unless their water conditions match those of their wild habitat. This is especially true not only with the chocolate gourami, but also with some of the more recently discovered bettas, which have yet to be bred in captivity over many generations, and so are currently less adaptable.

The size of the spawning set-up is obviously influenced by the species concerned, but bear in mind that although a pair may be persuaded to spawn successfully in a relatively small set-up, anabantoids

in general are prolific fish, with females often laying thousands of eggs at a single spawning. Hatching rates are generally high as well, and the young fish need plenty of space if they are subsequently to thrive, which is likely to mean dividing them up into a series of other aquariums as they grow older. A simple acrylic tank will make a suitable environment, and some of the designs on the market sold for herptiles can be useful, being relatively shallow and yet offering a good area for the young fish, as well as being equipped with an integral hood.

(!) GENTLE FILTRATION

Effective filtration is obviously important in the breeding tank, but avoid incorporating a power filter of any type, because of the relatively strong currents that will inevitably be produced. These are likely to destroy the bubblenest resulting in eggs and/or young fry being sucked up into the filter. Instead, use a sponge filter, coupled with regular water changes, to maintain water quality through the breeding and rearing period.

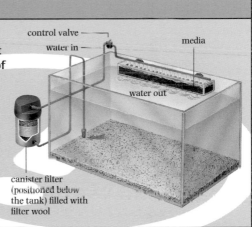

control valve
water in
media
water out
canister filter (positioned below the tank) filled with filter wool

ENCOURAGING SPAWNING BEHAVIOR

You can trigger reproductive activity in many anabantoids simply by increasing the live food component in their diet, rather than carrying out any drastic water changes. It is likely to take two or three weeks for this change to have a marked effect, with female fish appearing more swollen as the eggs develop in their bodies.

The water temperature is also significant, both in encouraging the onset of spawning activity and subsequently, the hatching and development of the young fish. The thermostat should be set to approximately 80°F (27°C). The spawning tank itself may be relatively bare, although the inclusion of floating plants such as hornwort (Ceratophyllum) may be recommended, especially for those anabantoids that incorporate pieces of vegetation into their nest. In other cases, a more heavily planted aquarium is advisable, with floating plants that cover the surface.

When attempting to breed Siamese fighting fish (Betta splendens), the male is usually placed in the spawning tank before the

➊ Small single-tray trickle filters sited above the tank can be used effectively on breeding and rearing tanks, or where it is impractical to fit a large multi-tray unit.

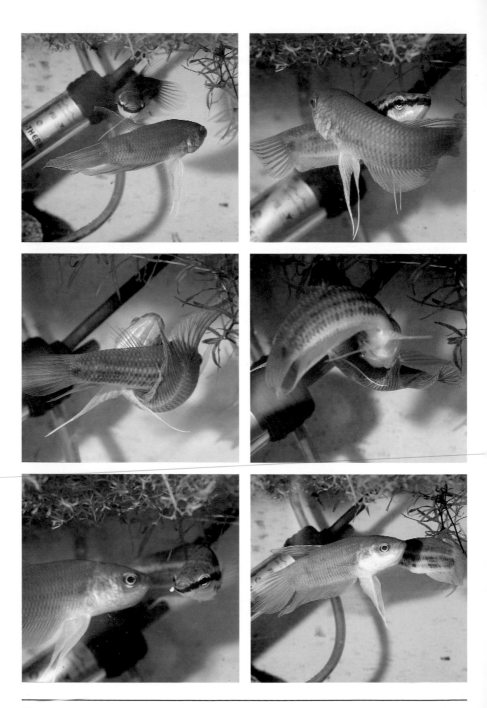

⬅ Spawning behavior in the brown mouthbrooder (*Betta fusca*); collecting the relatively few eggs that are produced by the female, avoiding any being lost. It is the male fish that care for the eggs in their mouths until the young can fend for themselves.

⬆ **Top** Some bushfish spawn in schools, with a variety of males fertilizing the eggs as these are laid. In such cases, where the eggs receive no parental care, females are generally larger than males. The reverse is usually the case in bubblenesting species.

⬆ **Above left and right** The male Day's spiketail (*Pseudosphromenus dayi*) usually builds the bubblenest not at the water surface but under an overhang or horizontal leaf. The male and sometimes also the female collect the sinking eggs.

A male Siamese fighting fish (*Betta splendens*) displaying to a female.

female, and then once he starts to construct the bubblenest, his intended partner can be introduced. The fish do not form a lasting pair bond, and in some cases, compatibility between the pair is a problem. It usually becomes evident quite soon after the introduction whether the fish are going to agree. If the male accepts his partner, then he is likely to allow her to approach, without being aggressive.

The timing of the introduction can be an important. Close examination of a female when she is ready to spawn reveals the development of her white egg-laying tube, known as an ovipositor. This looks rather like a small white pimple in the vent area. Once this is evident, then egg-laying is imminent.

DEALING WITH AGGRESSIVE BEHAVIOR

Older, fully mature Siamese fighting fish are often harder to pair up successfully than younger individuals. In cases where a male is known to be particularly aggressive, it may be worthwhile introducing several females in breeding condition to the tank at the same time, so as to divert his aggression away from one particular individual.

REPRODUCTIVE STRATEGIES

Mouthbrooding

Anabantoids have a number of different reproductive strategies, with the least prolific being the mouthbrooding bettas such as the painted betta (*Betta picta*). This method of caring for the fry places immediate restraints on the numbers that can be reared, yet it is also a relatively safe breeding strategy, being likely to yield a significant number of offspring. When spawning takes place, the eggs are trapped in the male's anal fin, being fertilized here. The female then collects the eggs in her mouth, preventing them being wafted away on currents, and transfers them to the male.

In some species, the female effectively spits the eggs out of her mouth in small batches, allowing the male to catch them in his mouth, but in other cases as with the Brunei beauty (*B. macrostoma*), she carefully transfers them directly to him from her mouth. It has been reported that some male bettas, and certainly the painted betta (*B. picta*), eat any surplus eggs produced by the female. This helps to sustain a male through his period of fasting until the young are released from his mouth approximately three weeks later. Although the female does not become involved in caring for her offspring, she remains in the vicinity of the male, seeking to drive off any potential predators that approach.

From the aquarist's viewpoint, these anabantoids are an ideal choice for breeding purposes, since not only are the fish themselves relatively small, attractive and easily accommodated in the home, but you are not swamped with huge numbers of offspring. Rearing is also much more straightforward, because of the relatively large size of the young fish, as they can be fed immediately on brine shrimp nauplii. As an example, painted bettas (*B. picta*) measure approximately 0.2in (7mm) long when they first need food whereas young Siamese fighting fish (*B. splendens*) fry are just 0.03in (1mm) in comparison.

Mouthbrooding is probably a relatively recent adaptation in anabantoids, being observed in comparatively few species. It has resulted in anatomical change, with the male's mouth becoming enlarged for the purpose. This is most evident when comparing members of the *Betta* genus that display this behavior with their bubblenesting relatives.

There has also been a corresponding shift in the actual pattern of mating behavior. The female often lies on her back, expelling the eggs while the male bends around her, so their genital orifices are effectively adjacent, maximizing the likelihood that the eggs will be fertilized. After this has occurred, both fish enter a temporary trancelike

◔ The painted betta (*Betta picta*) is a mouthbrooding species. The female collects the eggs after spawning, passing them to her mate.

state. In mouthbrooders, it is the female who wakes up first and starts to collect the eggs, in non-mouthbrooders the male generally carries out this task. Any eggs acquired by the female are likely to be eaten, which is one reason why pairs are usually separated, although subsequent aggressive behavior by the male can also necessitate this course of action.

It is not invariably the male anabantoid who displays mouthbrooding behavior—the female chocolate gourami (*Sphaerichthys osphromenoides*) is responsible for carrying the eggs and fry in this way, releasing them about two weeks after spawning occurred.

Egg-laying behavior patterns

Two broad categories exist within the egg-laying anabantoids. There are those that lay eggs that float up to the surface after spawning, while others produce eggs that sink. This is the result of differences in the constituents of their eggs, with floating eggs containing oil, which is lighter than water. Eggs that rise up to the surface are beneficial in areas where the water is naturally murky, as they can be located more easily, rather than disappearing out of sight.

There is perhaps more of a risk that these could fall victim to predators, and so anabantoids that produce floating eggs lay the largest numbers, typically between 1,000 and 20,000 in batches at a single spawning. This has an impact on the young fry, those hatching from floating eggs are smaller in size, having less food reserves within their yolk sacs. Eggs that sink are bigger, and the resulting offspring are usually able to eat slightly larger foods on hatching. This is because by the time they have exhausted their larger yolk sac reserves and start looking for food for the first time, they are older than the fry hatching from floating eggs.

Male anabantoids are often more closely involved with their offspring than female fish, but much depends on the species concerned. There are marked variations within the group. The kissing gourami (*Helostoma temminckii*) and various bushfish produce floating eggs in large numbers, which are simply carried on the currents and given no protection by either of the adult fish. Males in other egg-laying species build a bubblenest, as a refuge for their eggs. The construction of the nest by the male spotted

⬇ The eggs of the kissing gourami (*Helostoma temminckii*) float, which may help their dispersal and thus the survival of the young fish.

gourami (*Trichogaster trichopterus*) prior to spawning serves as a conditioning trigger, helping to stimulate the development of the female's eggs in her ovary.

This is a visual stimulus, but it is also clear that the male releases chemical messengers that help to stimulate egg-laying in the female. Females too release so-called pheromones, which indicate to a male whether or not they are ready to spawn, and so there is probably a fairly complex interaction between the sexes at this stage. Studies on *Trichogaster* spp. have shown that these pheromones register at the tips of their long, threadlike ventral fins. If these fins on the male are damaged or amputated, then they rarely attempt to construct a nest or spawn with a female, which suggests that the initial impetus to spawn comes from the female.

So the female may start the breeding cycle in the male fish, and then respond to his chemical messengers in the vicinity of the nest. Clearly, it is important to have mating and nest-building coordinated, because otherwise, eggs would be lost if there was no structure to house them.

The size of the nest is certainly a significant factor, because when it is relatively small, the number of eggs released by the female is correspondingly reduced. This may be the result of a feedback mechanism, because clearly there is little benefit in a female producing a large number of eggs if conditions at the outset are not favorable to the survival of the fry. The risk of eggs or young fry being lost from a small nest is increased if they are overcrowded at the outset. Not surprisingly, studies have also shown that the larger members of a species produce more offspring, although their nest size is not actually related to their body weight.

The reproductive feedback in those species that do not display any parental care is likely to be far less sophisticated. The more social natures of some African anabantoids has resulted in them spawning collectively. This has the advantage of overwhelming potential predators in the area with a food supply all at one time, so that a percentage of their eggs are destined to survive and hatch successfully.

⚠ CAREFUL CHOICE OF COMPANIONS

It is definitely not a good idea to house any of the so-called threadfin gouramis, including members of the genus *Colisa*, in a community aquarium alongside other fish, such as tiger barbs, which are likely to nip their fins. This could destroy their breeding potential in the future. In fact, gouramis are unlikely to breed successfully in a community aquarium.

Nest-building

The nest is constructed by the male fish drawing air into his mouth at the surface, and then spitting this out with mucus, creating small bubbles that adhere together to form a foam. This can become quite large reaching 20in (50cm) in diameter, although in other cases, the nest may be comprised of just a small number of bubbles.

Aquatic vegetation may be incorporated into the structure as well, affording extra stability, while the croaking gouramis (*Trichopsis* spp.) nest under the broad leaves of aquatic plants. Some anabantoids breed farther down in the water, finding a small cave for this purpose. This technique is favored by the spiketailed paradisefish (*Pseudosphromenus* spp.) and one of the less common *Betta* species, *B. smaragdina*.

↑ A bubblenest created by a male Siamese fighting fish (*Betta splendens*). Still water is essential as these nests are easily destroyed.

The smallest anabantoids avoid spawning in the open, where they are more vulnerable to predators. Instead, they retreat into relatively secure refuges—for example, the ornate gouramis (*Malpulutta kretseri*) utilize pieces of bamboo that they can just squeeze into. The licorice gourami (*Parosphromenus deissneri*) produces eggs that, under the soft water conditions found in its natural habitat, are adhesive by nature. They will stick to the small caves in which these fish retreat at spawning time. The actual color of the eggs is variable, and can be influenced by the diet of the fish, being reddish in some cases.

Spawning and nest guarding

Spawning is a protracted process that may take several hours, since the eggs are laid in a number of small batches—the Siamese fighting fish (*Betta splendens*) lays approximately 15 eggs in each batch. As the eggs sink, so the male has to retrieve them, transferring them to the bubblenest, the procedure being repeated until perhaps 600 or more eggs have been produced by the female.

It is usually advisable to remove the female after she has spawned, except in the cases where she normally plays a role in caring for the brood. The male normally remains in close attendance at the nest site, attempting to drive off any would-be predator, and retrieving any eggs or immobile young that drift out of the nest. This level of care lasts for about four days, by which time the young fry have hatched and he then loses interest in them, so he should

be transferred to another aquarium. There is no necessity to leave the male in attendance up to this point, but it is fascinating to watch his devoted behavior, and he may help to increase the number of fry that survive.

Rearing the fry

Young Siamese fighting fish (*Betta splendens*) and the other nest-building bettas are tiny when they first hatch, and they require suitably microscopic particles of food if they are to survive and grow through the early days of life. Although there are commercially available substitutes, it is not difficult to set up suitable cultures of infusoria to rear the fish. This can be achieved using chopped lettuce, with the leaves being placed in a jar of water and simply left to stand in a well-lit location. Once the water begins to turn slightly pink and cloudy, then the micro-organisms are replicating. It can then be transferred using eye drops into the aquarium.

If you prefer to rely on commercial substitutes, rotifers, a form of plankton, are available from some aquatic stores, while special foods sold for rearing young egg-layers are available. In an emergency, hard-boiled egg yolk sieved through muslin is another alternative, but this pollutes the water rapidly.

The early stages when the fry are free-swimming is a potentially difficult period during the breeding cycle—the young anabantoids must receive sufficient food, and yet this must not be wasted and cause a serious deterioration in water quality, which would be fatal to them. They cannot swim powerfully at first either, so the food particles need to be within easy reach. The young anabantoids need to be fed at least four times every day as a guide, with a water change carried out on alternate days, accounting for about a quarter of the total volume. It is vital that the dechlorinated water

⊙ Some anabantoids, such as the emerald betta (*Betta smaragdina*), seek out the added security of a cave or the underside of a leaf, and create their nest here.

added to the aquarium during a water change is at exactly the same temperature as that which has been siphoned out.

The fry should grow quickly, so they can be introduced to microworms and brine shrimp nauplii about four days after hatching, depending on the species. Do not suddenly switch their diet, as this can have a serious effect on the smaller individuals. With mouthbrooding bettas, the fry are usually large enough to take such live foods once they emerge from the male's mouth and therefore do not require infusoria.

DEVELOPMENT OF THE LABYRINTH ORGAN

This is the next critical phase in the growth of young anabantoids, which usually starts to occur when they are approximately three weeks old. It is vital that the tank hood is not left off now, because this will chill the water in contact with the air. This in turn will result in the production of mucus within the developing labyrinth organs, causing the young fish to die. This phase lasts about two weeks, and they will then be seen breathing air at the surface.

By this stage, the young fish are growing well, but they must not be overcrowded, because this is likely to lead to a serious fall-off in water quality, and increases the likelihood of them succumbing to environmental diseases such as fungus. In some cases, not all the young anabantoids grow at the same rate. This is quite normal, but in any brood, there are likely to be some weaklings that may display deformities, often handicapping their movement. They should be removed from the rearing tank, euthanasia the only option.

Although the largest species such as the giant gourami continue growing, albeit at a slower rate over the course of years, anabantoids generally display a fast growth spurt, which results in spotted gouramis (*Trichogaster trichopterus*) reaching nearly 3in (7.5cm) in length as early as three months of age, by which stage they are already sexually mature.

The appearance of some gouramis changes quite dramatically as they mature. The head of the young giant gourami (*Osphronemus goramy*) is pointed rather than rounded at this stage, while the gray body is banded with dark vertical stripes that later fade. These changes reflect different levels of threat for youngsters and adults, with the barring helping to provide disruptive camouflage, breaking up the body outline and concealing the fish more effectively while they are small.

⊘ AVOID CONFLICT

Especially with Siamese fighting fish (*Betta splendens*), young male fish, with their highly aggressive natures, need to be housed separately from each other by the time they are 12 weeks old. It is possible in some cases to keep a group of young male fish together for longer, provided that there is no disruption to the social hierarchy which will have evolved, but this remains fraught with danger.

COLOR-BREEDING IN *BETTA SPLENDENS*

At the core of the science of genetics is the fact that in any pair of alleles (any two or more genes that have the same relative position on the chromosomes and are responsible for alternative characteristics), one of the genes is likely to be dominant over the other, which means that in fish-keeping terms, the particular color or fin type that it is coding for will be manifested in the offspring. This gene is therefore dominant, whereas the other is described as recessive.

In most cases, the wild-type is dominant over any domesticated variants that arise, but unusually, this does not apply in Siamese fighting fish (*Betta splendens*). This means that the elaborate, long-finned characteristic is actually dominant over the sleeker short-finned variant. Nevertheless, such fish are far less equipped for survival in the wild because their more elaborate fins restrict their ability to swim fast, leaving them more vulnerable to predators as a result.

● Color and fin variants are now common in the Siamese fighting fish (*Betta splendens*).

The results of pairing a long-finned and short-finned individual together can be calculated quite simply, using the Punnett square system, which allows all the possible combinations of the alleles to be calculated. In the following example, EE represents the genes for the elaborate, long-finned characteristic, while ee is the code for a short-finned fish. The dominant character is recognizable because

⚠ LETHAL MUTATION

There is a lethal gene associated with black coloration in these fish, which means that pairing black individuals together may render the homozygous percentage of their offspring non-viable. Although there are different black strains, varying in their level of intensity in coloration, and the lethal factor does not apply in all cases, it is probably better to avoid combinations of this type if in doubt. Once identified, this particular dark strain can be crossed with blue fish, to prevent the problem of the lethal gene arising.

it is written in capitals. There are four possible combinations in this case, as is shown from the Punnett square system:

	E	E (Parent EE)
e	Ee	Ee
e (Parent ee)	Ee	Ee

This means that all the resulting offspring from this pairing will have elaborate long fins, but also carry the recessive "e" gene for the short fin characteristic. Since the genes do not correspond, these fry are described as "heterozygous," or sometimes as being "split" for the short-finned characteristic. This contrasts to the situation where the genes correspond, and they are then known as homozygous.

Much more variance in the progeny then results if these heterozygous fish are paired together, as shown from using the Punnett square system again:

	E	e (Parent Ee)
E	EE	Ee
e (Parent Ee)	Ee	ee

This then means that on average, out of any spawning, the progeny should be divided up in fin types as follows: one in four of the fry (ee) will be instantly distinguishable, thanks to their short fins. Half will be heterozygous (Ee), and these will be visually inseparable from the elaborate, homozygous long-finned individuals (EE) which comprise a further 25 percent of the total. The only way of differentiating between these two categories is to carry out further pairings. If just one short-finned individual crops up, this confirms that the fish are both heterozygous, since homozygous long-finned individuals cannot produce short-finned offspring.

Incomplete dominance

In some cases, the situation is more complex, notably where there are two different genes, with neither dominant, giving rise to what is called incomplete dominance. Heterozygous individuals differ from homozygous ones in their physical appearance or phenotype, as well as in their genetic makeup, or genotype. This makes them easier to identify, and plan for, in breeding programs. Cornflower-blue coloration in Siamese fighting fish (*B. splendens*) falls into this category, representing a combination of genes for steel-blue and green.

❺ The appearance of young anabantoids may change significantly as they grow older. Young mottled bushfish (*Ctenopoma weeksii*) are characterized by their black-and-white banding at first, before becoming more mottled, as seen here. Adult fish in contrast tend to be brownish, with a dark spot on each flank.

Color variants

Black is a relatively rare color, favored largely by specialist breeders, whereas brightly colored fish are seen in the pet trade. All are the result of different mutations exerting an effect on the pigments within a fish. In most cases, different varieties are described by their coloration, such as red, blue, or green. Those that have a patched appearance of light and dark areas may be known as marbled. "Cambodia" is the description given to the white strain. These fish can vary from semi-albino, distinguishable by their black eyes, which indicate they retain some color pigment in their bodies, through to pure red-eyed albinos. This name arose because when these rare fish were first seen in the West, they were thought to be a separate species, and named after the area of Southeast Asia where they reportedly occurred.

CHAPTER 6

Lifespan and Diseases

The fact that many anabantoids live under what would be perceived as less than optimal environmental conditions in the wild does not mean that in aquarium surroundings they are less susceptible to illness than other fish.

GENERAL PRECAUTIONS

⬇ Always check the fish each day for signs of illness. Sick individuals like this pearl gourami–so obviously "off-color"–represent a hazard to other fish.

It is important to ensure that regular water changes are carried out to safeguard the fish's well-being, and that the water quality is regularly monitored. Avoid overfeeding of the fish too, because this can lead to a rapid rise in nitrogenous waste, swamping the filtration system, as the uneaten food starts to decompose in the tank.

Seemingly innocuous household chemicals drawn into the aquarium via the air pump for example, even as vapors, can be fatal to fish,

and especially to anabantoids because they can breathe air. It is therefore most unwise to use any sprays in the same room as the aquarium, especially chemicals such as fly sprays, which almost certainly are harmful to the anabantoids. The solvents in paints, and tobacco smoke are potentially lethal to these fish.

In cases of poisoning, there is usually widespread and unexpected mortality, with most if not all of the fish dying suddenly. Any which are found alive are likely to be showing severe symptoms of respiratory distress. Transferring them elsewhere, in fresh dechlorinated water may mean they survive, but this depends on how much of the chemical has been absorbed into their bodies.

Anabantoids in general require a relatively high water temperature, and they suffer if exposed to cold conditions outside their normal temperature range. This can give rise to symptoms affecting the swim bladder as well as predisposing the fish to various opportunistic infections, their immune system being depressed as a result of the cold. In the event of a power out, there is little that can be done to maintain their water temperature, other than trying to insulate the aquarium to slow the rate of cooling. This can be achieved by wrapping a duvet or blanket around the tank, but first disconnect the power supply. Otherwise, if this comes back on in the middle of the night, there could be a fire risk.

PREVENTING DISEASE

There are a number of ways in which disease can enter the tank, but the most obvious is by introductions of new fish to an established set-up. This can always be a potential problem, even if the newcomer is disease-free, since the change in environment followed by possible bullying lowers its immunity to illness.

It is therefore important to keep new acquisitions isolated for several days, first so they can recover from the stress of the trip and also so you can check on their state of health. Signs of parasitic illness such as velvet disease (caused by *Oodinium*) may become apparent during this period, which would be harder to treat in the main aquarium, as well as representing an obvious hazard to the established fish.

A less obvious but equally serious potential hazard in the spread of disease can be aquarium nets. This is why when dealing with new individuals, a separate net should always be used rather than the one which is for catching fish in the main aquarium. After moving a sick fish, always leave the net to

> ## ① POWER OUT
>
> After a power failure, do not be tempted to rush to fill the tank with warm water once the electrical supply is restored. It is much less stressful for the fish if the water temperature is allowed to warm up slowly, rather than suddenly plunging them into a hot environment.

stand in a solution of special aquarium disinfectant as a further pre-cautionary measure. It is much easier to exclude disease in the first place, rather than trying to treat sick fish.

MANAGING SICKNESS

Parasitic illnesses

These are common in bettas and gouramis, with microscopic proto-zoa in particular being spread easily through the water. This is why if one fish in an aquarium is showing signs of infection, the rest are likely to be at risk. It is so easy to spread this type of infection by introducing a fish directly to an established aquarium, either when the parasites are present on the fish itself or in the accompanying droplets of water.

The good news, however, is that once the fish are established, then provided that they are kept isolated, the risk of these problems aris-ing is slight, although there is a possibility that such parasites could be introduced to the aquarium along with aquatic live foods.

One of the most common infections caused by protozoa, which are minute single-celled organisms, is the disease commonly known as white spot, and also as ick (ich), resulting from infection by *Ichthyophthirius multifiliis*. The name of this disease is derived from the presence of tiny white spots which cover the entire body of the fish. Each spot starts with the microscopic tomite burrowing in below the surface of the fish's body or gills, and feeding in its tissues. This then grows into the trophozoite stage in the parasite's lifecycle, which creates the distinctive white swelling.

These then rupture, releasing free-swimming tomites. The reason that this infection is potentially so serious in aquarium surroundings stems from the fact that each trophozoite may release up to 1,000 tomites. In the wild, many of these parasites would fail to find hosts and simply die, but within the confines of the aquarium they face no such difficulty, and infections prove overwhelming, especially for young anabantoids. The danger is not passed even once the tropho-zoite has ruptured, because the resulting wound on the fish's body is then vulnerable to attack by bacteria or fungi, or a combination of both, and this can subsequently prove to be fatal. Sequential infec-tions also occur, weakening the fish until ultimately it succumbs.

Unfortunately, the only stage in the lifecycle of this parasite which is visible is the trophozoite, which is why it is so important to check other fish in the tank for any signs of infection prior to purchase, with quarantine of new stock providing a secondary line of defense. When faced with an outbreak, the best thing to do is to move all the fish to a new aquarium, simply because if the tomites

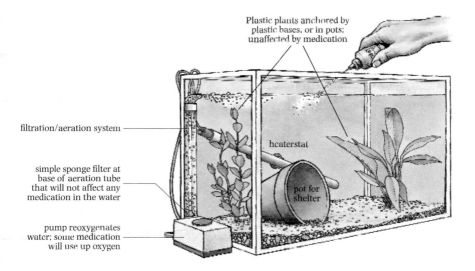

Plastic plants anchored by plastic bases, or in pots; unaffected by medication

filtration/aeration system

simple sponge filter at base of aeration tube that will not affect any medication in the water

pump reoxygenates water; some medication will use up oxygen

heaterstat

pot for shelter

fail to find a host within approximately 24 hours or so of hatching, then they will themselves die off.

Raising the water temperature helps, especially if you have removed the fish, because this speeds up the parasite's lifecycle, meaning that the tomites will die off more quickly in the absence of a host. There are also treatments available from aquarium stores and similar outlets that are effective at killing this free-living stage in its life-cycle.

Even carrying out a partial water change can help when faced with an outbreak, because this may reduce the risk of a secondary infection as well as eliminating some of the tomites from the tank. Anabantoids that are found in brackish water are less vulnerable to white spot than those kept in freshwater, because the parasite does not thrive in salty conditions.

Another major infection affecting anabantoids is velvet disease. The cause of this infection is another microscopic parasite, called *Oodinium pillularis*, which is quite unusual in its biology—it is part-plant, containing the plant pigment chlorophyll, which allows it to obtain energy by photosynthesis; but it also attacks fish, with bettas being especially vulnerable to this infection, also known as Colisa disease, because it was initially identified in those particular gouramis.

These parasites create a velvetlike, yellowish appearance, that can occur anywhere on the body and may also invade the digestive tract. One of the most obvious signs of an *Oodinium* infection is a change in the behavior of the fish because of the effects of the

⦿ A quarantine tank must supply the bare necessities. While it is difficult to prove that adding plastic plants helps the healing process it seems logical that it might benefit a stressed or injured fish.

resulting irritation. This causes them to start rubbing the affected areas of their bodies on decor in the tank in an attempt to relieve the discomfort.

Just as in an outbreak of white spot, *Oodinium* will spread rapidly in an aquarium, and if uncontrolled, it can cause heavy losses, especially in fry. There have been suggestions that it may lie dormant in some cases in the body, flaring up when the fish are under stress. It has been a particular problem associated with some of the rarer, recently discovered *Betta* species. Given the lifecycle of this parasite, it can also be introduced easily to the fish's environment with aquatic live food.

Again, it is possible to obtain proprietary treatments to overcome *Oodinium*, but carrying out water changes should also prove effective in controlling the spread of these parasites. When the fish are being housed singly in bowls rather than tanks, as is traditionally the case in Asia with Siamese fighting fish (*Betta splendens*), then once again, transferring the fish to a new bowl when the cysts have ruptured is important, as this should remove the majority of tomites from causing further harm, with treatment hopefully eliminating the remainder.

Clean surroundings are important, in order to prevent the risk of weakened fish succumbing to fungal or bacterial disease. Other protozoa have been recorded as causing illness in anabantoids, but they can usually be controlled in a similar way. If faced with a bad outbreak, seek the advice of an experienced fish veterinarian, who should be able to identify the particular protozoan involved.

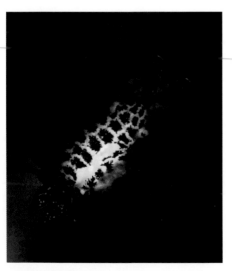

⬇ A magnified view of a fish louse (*Argulus*). These parasites cause irritation that can lead to a generalized infection.

Some larger parasites may afflict anabantoids on occasions, but these are relatively rare, and should be dealt with by a responsible outlet prior to the fish being put on sale. Nevertheless, there is a slight risk that the fish could encounter these parasites in a store tank, with fish lice (*Argulus*) being among the most common. In spite of their name, these are crustaceans, with a flat, disklike shape, measuring about 0.3in (0.6cm) in diameter. Fish lice anchor on to the fish's body, again causing irritation and leading to the fish scraping against the decor in the aquarium, as well as clamping its fins in some cases. These symptoms can be linked with other infections though, and it is necessary to catch the fish and examine it closely in order to spot the parasites.

Do not be tempted to pull off the louse with a pair of tweezers, as this will worsen the situation. Instead, obtain a suitable medication and make a bath for the anabantoid. This can be created using a large, clean, empty plastic container, such as a disused ice cream tub, but first, rinse this out thoroughly to remove any residual traces of dishwashing liquid or powder that could be harmful to the fish. Then be sure to keep the container covered with a secure lid while the fish is being treated, so as to prevent any risk of it jumping out, or it falling victim to a pet cat in the home. The sooner that treatment begins, the greater will be the likelihood of success, before the fish is badly weakened. There is little risk of *Argulus* breeding in the home aquarium, but infections can develop at the site where they attached to the body.

Flukes are also quite rare in anabantoids, but while skin flukes may be clearly evident, those under the gills are more likely to be revealed by a change in the fish's behavior. It will have obvious difficulty in breathing, with the movement of the gill covers being faster than usual. Closer examination here can reveal the presence of the parasites themselves, which cause intense irritation in this area of the body. Again, a treatment bath is required.

> ### ⓘ CAREFUL DOSING
>
> **When making up medication for your anabantoids, always be sure to follow the instructions closely, and do not forget to dechlorinate the water and check the temperature before transferring the fish, if using a separate bath for them. It is also important not to leave the fish in the bath for longer than directed, simply because this itself may be fatal, given their weakened condition and the inevitable toxic nature of the chemical concerned.**

Bacterial diseases

There can be other causes of inflamed gills, such as bacterial disease. This should be suspected if there is no obvious sign of parasites. It may be a localized problem, but is often linked with a more generalized bacterial infection, resulting in septicemia.

Treatment under these circumstances is often difficult, largely because the infection is often well advanced and attacking the internal body organs before signs become apparent. Red streaking externally, on the body or fins for example, is generally associated with this condition, although it may not be evident on a dark-colored anabantoid.

A generalized bacterial infection can often be linked with preceding damage to the scales, allowing harmful bacteria to breach the body's defenses, which is why it is important to handle fish carefully to avoid causing any injury. Never be tempted to touch a fish directly with dry hands, for example, because this will damage the outer protective mucus covering the body. Parasites too can have the same effect, and may lead indirectly to the death of fish. Treatment of septicemia is frequently unsuccessful, although antibiotic baths, and even injections in larger individuals, can sometimes prove to be worthwhile. Early diagnosis of the problem is more significant in determining whether the fish lives or dies.

❺ This spotted gourami (*Trichogaster trichopterus*) has very indistinct spots and the scales have become mottled and darker; but he is as fit as he could be. The changes are due simply to old age. At three years old, he is a senior citizen.

Other disorders

Although the signs of dropsy are obvious—a swollen abdomen, with the scales being pushed away from the body, creating what is sometimes described as a pine cone effect—there is no single cause. It can be the result of a localized bacterial infection attacking the kidneys and leading to renal failure. Treatment is unlikely to be successful, especially in the latter stages of the illness, but occasionally antibiotic therapy can lead to recovery. In cases of noninfectious dropsy where the cause is unclear, there is little that can be done. The fish's condition will deteriorate, and euthanasia is the only option.

The swim bladder has an important role to play in regulating the fish's buoyancy, as well as providing an auxiliary supply of oxygen as necessary. On occasions, however, problems arise, especially in young anabantoids, with the result that the fish are unable to swim properly, so they lie either on the bottom or hang at an unusual angle in the water.

A sudden falloff in water temperature may be a cause of this problem in young anabantoids, although it can also be an individual developmental abnormality. In older fish, it is regarded as a sign of senility. Anabantoids as a group do not have a long lifespan, especially smaller members of the group, with Siamese fighting fish (*Betta splendens*), for example, being unlikely to live more than two or three years. Larger gouramis such as the giant gourami (*Osphronemus goramy*) may, however, live for five years or so.

In some young fish, there may be an underlying anatomical reason, arising from domestication. The risk of this disorder occurring is greater in Siamese fighting fish (*Betta splendens*) that have double tails, simply because their bodies are shorter, and this has distorted the development of the swim bladder. There is no clear evidence that the underlying cause of the problem is strictly genetic, but it does appear to be linked with the change in body shape. Unfortunately, there is usually little that can be done for a swim bladder disorder, although occasionally, a bacterial infection may be blamed for the condition and treatment is possible. In a few cases, fish may recover spontaneously within a short time, notably if they have become chilled. Otherwise, affected individuals will need to be painlessly killed—a task that can be carried out by your veterinarian if you wish.

Bacterial and fungal disease are confused in so-called mouth fungus, which is frequently seen around the mouth of fish. While appearing rather like fungus, it is the result of an infection by *Flexibacter* bacteria and can be treated successfully with a proprietary remedy.

Fungal disease

Most fungal infections affecting anabantoids are opportunistic by nature. This is because under normal circumstances, the fish's immune system prevents an infection of this type becoming established. If the individual anabantoid is already weakened, as the result of a parasitic illness for example, then the risk of fungal disease is dramatically increased. This occurs as a result of the presence of fungal spores in the water that can then overwhelm the body's defenses at the site of the injury. The typical whitish, haloed appearance associated with fungal disease then becomes apparent.

Older and younger anabantoids are more vulnerable to fungal illness, since their ability to fight opportunistic infections of this type is less effective. Physical characteristics of anabantoids

🔾 Fungal disease is often linked with damage to the fins or body, and requires rapid treatment to prevent it spreading further.

can also have an impact on their susceptibility to fungal infections. Long-finned individuals such as the ornamental forms of the Siamese fighting fish (*Betta splendens*) are particularly vulnerable to suffering from attacks of this type on their fins, the initial cause in this case being poor water quality.

In the early stages, the fins may start to appear frayed and inflamed at their edges, gradually becoming more obviously eroded. Bacterial infections may gain a hold here too, and it is vital to take action to prevent further damage to the fins without delay. Not only does this mean that affected individuals should recover quickly, but it also ensures that the risk of a more generalized infection is reduced. Improving the environmental conditions by carrying out more regular and extensive water changes helps, while there are various proprietary remedies that can be used to treat fungal infections successfully. In cases where there is a fungal infection within the body that is attacking the body organs, treatment is likely to be impossible, although luckily, this type of infection is extremely rare. Loss of weight and a roughened skin are typical symptoms.

Dietary problems and pop-eye

It is not uncommon for anabantoids to suffer occasionally from constipation. This is often linked to feeding the fish mainly on dry food, and it can be corrected by adding live food to their diet in some guise on a regular basis. Signs of constipation are vague, although the

> (!) **TREATMENT CONCERNS**
>
> A number of the traditional remedies used to treat fish ailments are based on dyes such as methylene blue. Beware of using these in a glass tank, the panels of which are held together with silicone sealant, because the silicone is likely to be permanently stained by the dye.
>
> It is also important to bear in mind that the presence of any carbon—either on its own or integrated into a filter pad—is likely to deactivate most treatments rapidly. This is why direct medication of affected individuals is often more satisfactory, while removing them to a treatment tank helps to safeguard the health of other fish that are housed alongside them.

most obvious—a lack of appetite—is clear-cut, even if not diagnostic. You may notice a slight swelling around the vent area with the fish appearing agitated. Long strands of fecal material hanging out of the vent also help to indicate this condition.

The condition known as pop-eye or exophthalmia can also be linked to diet, suggestive of a deficiency in Vitamin A, although this is unlikely if the anabantoids are receiving a formulated food, provided that the recommended use-by date has not been passed. Protruding eyes may also crop up occasionally for genetic reasons, but other causes such as a tumor or an infection should be suspected, depending partly on whether one or both eyes are affected.

Human health concerns

Exophthalmia can also be a symptom linked with piscine tuberculosis, which is a serious condition. This is a chronic wasting disease, causing affected fish to lose condition and color. It can also represent a hazard to people, it can enter the skin through cuts or abrasions, creating a swelling known as a granuloma at the point of entry.

In order to protect yourself against the *Mycobacterium* responsible, or indeed other potentially harmful microbes such as *Vibrio* bacteria that may be present in the aquarium water, it is sensible to wear a clean pair of gloves whenever delving into the tank for any reason. Never wash these off with soap or use them for other purposes though, as you could end up inadvertently poisoning the fish. Fish suffering from piscine tuberculosis should be put to sleep, and their quarters should be stripped down completely and disinfected thoroughly before restocking occurs.

CHAPTER 7

Popular Anabantoids

FAMILY BELONTIIDAE

★ SIAMESE FIGHTING FISH

Betta splendens

Distribution: Southeast Asia, centered on Thailand but the precise natural distribution of these fish is unclear, because they have been introduced to many separate localities in the region. The discovery of closely related species in Thailand supports the view that the original natural distribution of these fish was relatively small, being restricted just to northern, western, and central areas of the country.

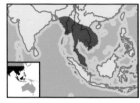

Size: Up to 2.5in (6cm).

Form: The wild form of the Siamese fighting fish is far removed from its domesticated cousin, with the ancestral form being short-finned, compared with the elaborate flowing fins associated with the universally kept and highly colorful veiled form that is a product of centuries of selective breeding. Females have the rounded fin shape of their ancestor, with the long dorsal and anal fins of male fish allowing the sexes to be distinguished easily.

Diet: Will eat flake and small live foods readily.

Natural habitat and behavior: These bettas naturally inhabit shallow stretches of water, such as ditches, paddy fields, and even the *klongs* or canals that flow through towns. The wild form of this species is essentially unknown in the aquarium hobby today, even in its homeland where these fish are popular. They are known locally as pla-kat, which translates as the "biting and tearing fish," reflecting the highly aggressive behavior of the males. Their

territorial instincts are such that they will fight to the death in a confined space such as an aquarium, but in the wild, after ritualistic displays, the weaker individual retreats from conflict.

Aquarium conditions: The aggressive nature of males of this species has meant that they are often confined in small containers that afford little space for swimming, and placing them in receptacles in close proximity to each other means they are displaying and under constant stress at the same time. Males must not be housed together in aquarium surroundings, and although they can be kept individually within a community setup, the choice of tankmates needs to be considered carefully. A male Siamese fighting fish suffers badly if kept in an aquarium alongside more agile, fin-nipping species such as tiger barbs (*Barbus tetrazona*). Equally, it is not recommended to house a red example alongside fish displaying similar coloration, such as a red-tailed black shark (*Labeo bicolor*), because the betta might then decide to harry and attack its companion. Although Siamese fighting fish favor soft and slightly acidic water conditions, their most important requirement is the temperature of the water. This needs to be maintained between 75–86°F (24–30°C).

For breeding purposes, a male should be housed in the company of several females, in a tank where the water level has been lowered to about 6in (15cm). The aquarium must still remain covered to maintain the air temperature. The female swells with spawn as the time for breeding approaches, with the male constructing the bubblenest between the floating plants at the surface. After spawning has occurred, the male collects the eggs and transfers them to the rather delicate bubblenest, often assisted for a time by the female, until she is driven away by her mate. The whole process takes about two hours.

The fry are free-swimming about four days after laying took place. Water quality is important during the rearing period. The sexes can be distinguished once the young bettas are between two and three months old.

⭐ SLENDER BETTA

Betta bellica

Distribution: Southeast Asia, originally from the Perak region of Malaysia, but now more widely distributed on peninsular Malaysia and also present on Sumatra. The species is now generally regarded as synonymous with *B. fasciata*.

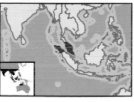

Size: Between 4–5in (10–12.5cm).

Form: One of the biggest members of its genus, with the more colorful males attaining a larger size than females, and developing more elaborate fins—their caudal fins develop a naturally spiky appearance, compared with those of females. The coloration of both sexes is similar, being yellowish-brown on the front part of the body, with evident bluish-green scaling becoming prominent along its length, extending to the fins.

Diet: Eats a wide range of prepared foods. Small invertebrates should feature in their diet, but large earthworms should be avoided, as reports suggest that fish may choke on them.

Natural habitat and behavior: Occurs in water that is naturally soft and acidic, with a typical temperature of 82°F (28°C). Often associated with peat swamp forests. Primarily insectivorous, with dragonfly larvae featuring prominently in the diet of these fish in the wild. They may occasionally clamber out on to leaves of plants growing at the water's surface.

Aquarium conditions: In spite of the warlike epithet of its scientific name "bellica," this is a generally peaceful species, although males can become highly aggressive toward each other when breeding. Water conditions should match those in the wild, with retreats being created by dense planting and the inclusion of bogwood. The aquarium should incorporate some floating plants, and so must not be filled to the top. It needs to be kept covered, because these bettas can easily jump out of the water. After spawning, the male carries the eggs to the nest, with the young hatching about a day later, although it takes three days for them to absorb their yolk sacs and start to swim freely around their quarters. They need to be reared on a suitable fry food at first. This is quite a challenging bubblenesting species to breed successfully.

Betta pugnax

Distribution: Southeast Asia, occurring over the entire Malaysian peninsula south of Thailand. Also occurs on the adjacent island of Penang.

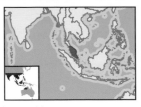

Size: Up to 4.75in (12cm).

Form: Slender body, with a powerful head. Basic color scheme is brown with greenish-blue iridescence extending from the lower jaw across the gill covers along the lower part of the body, but this pattern is quite variable. Females and young fish have two dark bars running down each side of the body, augmented by corresponding head stripes.

Diet: Insectivorous, so offer live foods in various forms, although they also feed on standard fare.

Natural habitat and behavior: Occurs in mountain streams, where the water is clear and fast-flowing, although these bettas tend to occupy areas of aquatic vegetation where the current is not as strong, adjacent to the banks. Seasonal water flows affect the temperature of their environment. At peak flow rates, this may measure just 72°F (22°C), but when the current is slower, this can rise to 79°F (26°C). As its name says, this particular species is a mouthbrooder rather than a bubblenester.

Aquarium conditions: Water quality is important, and the filtration system must be efficient, since these bettas are relatively unusual in not inhabiting sluggish stretches of water. Being used to rain-fed streams, they require soft water conditions, with a slightly acidic pH, and should be housed in a well-planted tank to match their natural habitat. The water level can be relatively shallow, being lowered to as little as 4in (10cm) when spawning is anticipated. Spawning itself is a protracted process, which may take as long as five hours, with the male retaining the eggs in his mouth until the fry hatch and emerge into the aquarium about 10 days later. They can be reared successfully on brine shrimp nauplii from the outset.

⬆ Dwarf Penang mouthbrooder   ⬇ Bukit Merah mouthbrooder

⭐ WINE RED FIGHTER (CLARET BETTA)

Betta coccina

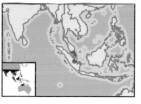

Distribution: Southeast Asia, in southern peninsular region of Malaysia, notably from Muar, and also from near Jambi in central Sumatra.

Size: Up to 2.25in (5.5cm).

Form: A beautiful, relatively narrow-bodied betta, with a somewhat variable reddish-brown body color and paler longitudinal stripes. Males display a dark spot on the flanks with bluish-green iridescence, and bluish-white edging to their dorsal and caudal fins.

Diet: Live foods, fresh, freeze-dried, and deep frozen.

Natural habitat and behavior: Found in both clear as well as blackwater stretches of water, colored by tannins, where the water temperature is 77–81°F (25–27°C).

Aquarium conditions: Soft, acidic water conditions, with a pH of around 4.5, are required by these bettas, with dense planting being required to reduce the risk of aggressive encounters. They are quite agile fish by nature, and must be kept in a covered aquarium because they can jump out quite easily. A blackwater extract can be added to the water. When claret bettas come into spawning condition, the females develop a greenish stripe down the sides of their bodies, whereas the distinctive flank marking of the male is edged with white. They lay relatively small batches, typically between 30–60 eggs in bubblenests that are smaller than 2in (5cm) in diameter. The fry are generally quite delicate, and, like the adults, can be vulnerable to velvet disease (see pages 105–6). They can be reared on a proprietary rearing food and infusoria at first, before being introduced to brine shrimp nauplii. It is possible to leave these bettas together as a family group, as the adults do not usually harm their offspring, with the young bettas being removed by the time they are two months old. Those spawning in their first year produce relatively small broods.

Betta persephone

Distribution: Southeast Asia, present around Muar and other localities in southern Malaysia.

Size: No larger than 1.5in (4cm).

Form: Predominantly brown to blackish body coloration, with dark greenish-blue fins and blue on the iris. The coloration of the male becomes more intense at the start of the breeding period, with the larger size of the male's dorsal and caudal fins also helping to distinguish the sexes.

Diet: Fresh and packaged live foods of suitable size.

Natural habitat and behavior: A reclusive species, found in shallow stretches of water in tropical forest. Its small size undoubtedly aids its survival, helping these fish to live in little more than puddles on occasions, and hide under leaves and roots in this type of environment. Its distribution is strongly influenced by rainfall, and not surprisingly, these bettas live in soft and yet acidic water conditions. It is reputed to occur in the company of the wine red fighter (*B. coccina*) near Muar.

Aquarium conditions: It is usually recommended to accommodate black bettas in densely planted aquariums, as single pairs. The pH should be maintained at about 5.0, with the water being filtered through aquarium peat. Black bettas are bubblenesters, with females laying small numbers of eggs, typically no more than 40 at a spawning. The young need to be reared on infusoria, rotifers, or similar tiny foodstuffs until they have been free-swimming for about a week, when brine shrimp nauplii can be introduced to their diet. In spite of their small size, these bettas mature slowly, being unlikely to breed for the first time until they are nine months old. Up until this stage, it is usually possible to leave them with the adult fish, assuming that they are housed in a spacious aquarium, although males become territorial as they mature, and need to be separated by this stage.

★ PEACEFUL BETTA (CRESCENT BETTA)

Betta imbelis

Distribution: Southeast Asia, including the Malay peninsula, the island of Phuket off southern Thailand, northeastern Sumatra and western Borneo.

Size: Up to 2in (5cm).

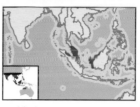

Form: Males have a blackish or blue body coloration overall, with a greenish sheen like verdigris over the gill covers. The caudal fin has a deep red crescent-shaped marking on it, which is especially prominent when they are in breeding condition, with an outer black band. The body coloration of females is brown, acquiring a lighter, more yellowish cross-banding when they are in breeding condition. Their fins are smaller in overall size and, although marked with blue and red, are less colorful. The depth of coloration also varies according to the population concerned.

Diet: Prepared foods such as flake, plus live foods.

Natural habitat and behavior: Usually occurring in shallow areas of water, these bettas are sometimes encountered in rice paddies, as well as ditches and ponds. They are found in association with aquatic vegetation, where they can conceal themselves from potential predators, even where the water level is low. Peaceful bettas are a bubblenesting species, with courtship being much more gentle than in other members of this group. Spawning typically takes two hours, with the female remaining virtually motionless for part of this time, allowing the male to collect the eggs, numbering up to 15, once he breaks free from her. She may help to gather them as well, spitting them out to her mate close to the nest.

Aquarium conditions: As its name suggests, this species is peaceful by nature, and so it is possible to house several pairs together in the same aquarium, although it is likely to be hazardous to introduce another male into an established group. Some disputes may occur close to a bubblenest created by a male but these territorial arguments do not result in serious fighting. Rearing requirements of the young are similar to those of other bubblenesting bettas.

Belontia signata

Distribution: The island of Sri Lanka, off India's southeastern coast.

Size: Up to 6in (15cm) but typically smaller.

Form: The distinctive rays present on the caudal fin of mature individuals of this species, resembling the teeth of a comb, are responsible for its common name. Combtails are not especially colorful fish, being pale yellowish-brown with more silvery underparts. Sexing is relatively difficult, although males may be distinguished by having a longer dorsal fin. A localized form is the pectoral spot combtail (*B. s. jonklaasi*), so called because of the area of darker coloration on this area of the body.

Diet: Omnivorous, eating both prepared foods and live food.

Natural habitat and behavior: These paradisefish are shy and retiring by nature. They occur not just in slow-flowing streams but also rivers in the lowlands of their native island, hiding near the banks among aquatic vegetation. A distinctive, dark-colored

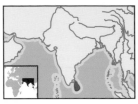

morph inhabits the streams that flow through the dense and gloomy Kottawa Forest in southwestern Sri Lanka.

Aquarium conditions: Subdued lighting, and a well-planted tank with a dark substrate helps to replicate the natural environment of these fish. Water conditions should be soft, with a pH around neutral, and a temperature between 74–82°F (24–28°C). Unfortunately, combtails can prove rather disruptive and even aggressive on occasions, and so companions for them need to be chosen carefully. Kissing gouramis (*Helostoma temminckii*) will be suitable. Once individuals reach about 3.5in (9cm) in length, they are mature. The nest is not an elaborate construction, but may be comprised of just a single bubble trapped under a plant leaf at the time of spawning. The young are slow to develop, only becoming free-swimming about six days after spawning, but they are large enough to be reared directly on brine shrimp nauplii. Unusually, both the adult fish watch over the brood, for as long as six weeks.

⭐ PARADISEFISH

Macropodus opercularis

Distribution: Eastern Asia, including southern China, Korea, Vietnam, Taiwan and neighboring islands, including the Ryukyu group.

Size: Males up to 4.75in (12cm) with females being smaller.

Form: Distinctive alternating orange-red and blue vertical bands running vertically down both sides of the body, with black markings too, notably on the head. A prominent bluish spot is present on the gill plates. The fins are long and flowing, especially in the male, with the caudal fin in particular looking uneven at its tip, thanks to the extensions present on the rays.

Diet: Eats both prepared foods and live foods readily.

Natural habitat and behavior: Found in a wide range of habitats from paddy fields to streams and even sometimes brackish waters. Ranging farther north than other species, these fish can be found in waters that may dip down to 50°F (10°C) or even lower during the winter, and rise up to 95°F (35°C) in the summer period.

Aquarium conditions: Paradisefish are robust, with males being aggressive, to the extent they must be kept apart from each other. They need a spacious, well-planted aquarium, so that females can retreat from the close attention of the male.

Floating plants at the surface are recommended, with a site under a leaf often being chosen by the male to construct a bubblenest. Although paradisefish can be kept in the home without any artificial heat, increasing the water temperature typically up to around 82°F (28°C) and lowering the water level slightly should serve as spawning triggers, as will increasing the amount of live food in the diet. Females may lay up to 500 eggs, with the male watching over the brood as the young hatch and develop. Infusoria should be offered as their first food. With so many potential fry, good filtration and regular partial water changes are essential. This species hybridizes easily with its two closest relatives, *M. concolor* (black paradisefish) and *M. ocellatus* (Chinese paradisefish).

Malpulutta kretseri

Distribution: Asia, occurring in western Sri Lanka.

Size: Up to 3.5in (9cm) but typically less than 2.5in (6cm).

Form: Variable—pale salmon-pink body coloration, with darker markings, and bluish coloration on

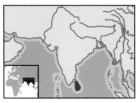

the fins, with darker spots. Males easily identifiable by their tapering dorsal fin as well as the long central rays of their caudal fins, which are almost 1in (2.5cm) long. Blue coloration is especially pronounced in the subspecies described as *M. k. minor*, with some individuals displaying a more violet hue.

Diet: Small live foods and prepared diets.

Natural habitat and behavior: Inhabits dark, shaded waters within the Kottawa Forest Reserve, often hiding in among accumulations of dead leaves. These gouramis stay close into the bank, being protected by overhanging vegetation. They are not common in the wild, but a government-approved breeding project has been established to ensure, it is hoped, that stocks can be maintained in aquariums around the world.

Aquarium conditions: The tank water needs to be soft and acidic, with the aquarium well planted. Ornate gouramis are quite delicate fish, and effective filtration is essential to prevent any accumulation of nitrogenous waste, which would adversely affect their health. Breeding too is often problematic. The bubblenest is located quite close to the floor of the aquarium, sometimes located in a retreat or under a broad leaf. Both fish sink to the floor of the tank after spawning, with the female collecting the eggs, and the male then guards the nest site and subsequently watches over the young. The hatching period is relatively long, typically taking 2.5 days, and it is vital to ensure the water temperature does not fluctuate significantly during this period. It should correspond to that of their natural habitat, being 81°F (27°C). Infusoria or a similar food is initially required for successful rearing of the fry.

⬆ Ornate gourami male   ⬇ Ornate gourami female

⭐ SPIKE-TAILED PARADISEFISH (RED-EYE SPIKETAIL)

Pseudosphromenus cupanus

Distribution: Southeastern India and Sri Lanka. May also occur farther east.

Size: Up to 2.5in (8cm).

Form: Predominantly coppery-brown, with bluish edging to the fins, especially the caudal. Although

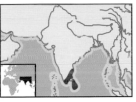

the extension forming a characteristic spike on the caudal fin tends to be a feature of males, this characteristic is also shared with some females. When in breeding condition, males develop their distinctive bright red iris, and similar coloration on the pectoral and anal fins, while females darken in color, becoming blackish.

Diet: Omnivorous, eating both prepared foods and live foods.

Natural habitat and behavior: These fish inhabit slowly flowing streams and ditches, sometimes in rainforest surroundings as well as agricultural areas, such as paddy fields. Generally, they seek out darkened environments, where they can hide among aquatic vegetation.

Aquarium conditions: Ideal conditions for these fish consist of a dark base to the aquarium, which can be created by suitable gravel, and retreats formed not just by plants but other decor such as bogwood. They are quite undemanding in their water chemistry needs, and can adapt to water temperatures ranging from just 68°F (20°C) to 82°F (28°C). Spike-tailed paradisefish are peaceful by nature, and should only be kept in pairs with gentle, quiet companions of unrelated species. Increasing the water temperature and live food component in the diet should trigger spawning behavior. The bubble-nest may be built under vegetation, or elsewhere, even sometimes within a flowerpot. The entire spawning process lasts about four hours, with the young fish hatching within 48 hours. Around four days after spawning, they start to become free-swimming and can be reared on infusoria at first. There is generally no need to remove their parents from the aquarium. Even when the male is guarding the nest, he is unlikely to be aggressive to his partner.

Trichogaster leerii

Distribution: Southeast Asia, present in peninsular Malaysia, possibly extending to Thailand. Also present on Sumatra, Borneo, and perhaps Java.

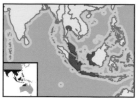

Size: Up to 6in (15cm) but usually smaller.

Form: Beautiful pale whitish-blue spots on the sides of the body, extending to the fins, with a black stripe passing through the eyes along the body to the base of the caudal fin. Mature males have longer, more-pointed dorsal and anal fins, as well as a reddish area extending over the lower part of the face. A male in breeding condition is unforgettable.

Diet: Will take both prepared foods and live foods.

Natural habitat and behavior: These beautiful fish inhabit shallow, flowing streams running through areas of rain forest. Unfortunately, males are quite slow to develop their distinctive coloration, and sexing is unlikely to be possible until they have reached a length of approximately 3in (8cm).

Aquarium conditions: To replicate their natural habitat, an aquarium for pearl gouramis should be filled to only 12in (30cm), with well-filtered, soft, slightly acidic water. The water temperature should be 74–82°F (24–28°C). A dense covering of floating plants is recommended, with subdued lighting. Pearl gouramis are usually quite peaceful fish, but companions for them should be chosen carefully. Barbs are not recommended because of their tendency to engage in fin-nipping, but tetras are likely to be suitable. For breeding purposes, the depth of water needs to be halved, and the water temperature raised close to 86°F (30°C). The male creates a large bubblenest and displays beneath it to the female. Both parents collect the eggs. He guards them until they hatch after one day. A large aquarium is essential for breeding purposes, and should be at least 40in (100cm) long, given that the brood may comprise nearly 1,000 young fry. The fry require small foods such as paramecium at first.

⬆ Pearl gourami   ⬇ Pearl gourami male in breeding condition

★ MOONLIGHT GOURAMI

Trichogaster microlepis

Distribution: Southeast Asia, present in Cambodia (Kampuchea), Thailand, and Malaysia.

Size: Up to 8in (20cm) but usually much smaller.

Form: Shimmering silvery coloration, with a slight greenish hue especially in males. Males can also be distinguished by the orange-red coloration in the vicinity of the chest, which extends along their long, narrow pelvic fins, and the elongated, pointed shape of the dorsal fin. The red marking on the upper part of the iris occurs in both sexes.

Diet: Eats both prepared foods and live food.

Natural habitat and behavior: These shy gouramis occur in both slow-flowing and stationary stretches of water, and may even enter flooded paddy fields on occasions. Aquatic vegetation at the surface is important, providing anchorage points for their bubblenests. They may even nibble at the leaves of fine-leaved plants, and incorporate these pieces into the construction of the nest itself.

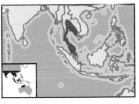

Aquarium conditions: These gouramis require a relatively large, well-planted aquarium, which should incorporate floating plants or those such as *Nymphaea* species whose leaves spread above the water surface. A water temperature of 79–86°F (26–30°C) is ideal, and the pH should be between slightly acidic and neutral, with soft water conditions being preferable. Moonlight gouramis are quite shy and timid fish, and any companions need to be chosen carefully, particularly to prevent damage to their modified pelvic fins. Dwarf cichlids or tetras are normally suitable. When breeding is imminent, lower the water level, with a slight increase in water temperature often providing the necessary trigger. At this stage, males construct a large bubblenest that may extend nearly 1in (2.5cm) above the surface of the water. The young gouramis are free-swimming within four days following egg-laying. They need a plentiful supply of infusoria at first, being transferred across to brine shrimp nauplii as they grow older.

Trichogaster trichopterus

Distribution: Southeast Asia, occurring over a wide area from Indochina to Thailand, Malaysia, Indonesia, and offshore islands.

Size: Up to 6in (15cm), although usually smaller.

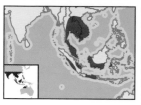

Form: The appearance of these gouramis differs through their range. The form found on Sumatra is known as the blue gourami (*T. t. sumatranus*). It is less of a grayish shade and also grows slightly smaller than its mainland cousin—the two distinctive black spots on each side of the body are still evident, however. Males can be distinguished by the pointed tip to their dorsal fin. Over recent years, color hybrids have become more common in the hobby, with the golden form in particular proving popular. The so-called "cosby" variant is also widely kept, displaying more prominent dark blue markings on its body than the true spotted gourami.

Diet: Exceedingly easy to cater for, eating almost anything.

Natural habitat and behavior: These gouramis rank as probably the most adaptable of all species, and they are even farmed as food in some parts of their range. They can be found in muddy forest streams and in the clear waters of paddy fields.

Aquarium conditions: This species is quite undemanding in its water chemistry requirements, and survives well at temperatures in the range of 72–82°F (22–28°C). It does require a large aquarium, especially for breeding, because in common with related gouramis, these fish are highly prolific. In addition, males construct bubblenests which may be up to 10in (25cm) in diameter. It may well be necessary to remove the female after spawning, as the male can become aggressive toward her. Males should be kept apart from each other, but overall, these gouramis are not aggressive fish and adults especially can prove shy and retiring for a time when moved from familiar surroundings.

🔽 Blue marble cosby gourami (*Trichogaster trichopterus* "cosby")

➡ Opaline gourami (*Trichogaster trichopterus* "opal")

⭐ SNAKESKIN GOURAMI

Trichogaster pectoralis

Distribution: Southeast Asia, being naturally present in Cambodia (Kampuchea), Thailand and the Malay peninsula. Introduced to Sri Lanka and elsewhere. These fish are valued in Asia as a source of food, and have been widely introduced outside their native range for this purpose.

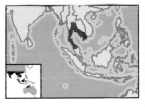

Size: Up to 8in (20cm) but usually smaller.

Form: This gourami is so called because of its snakelike body patterning, although this can be influenced both by the fish's mood and the lighting conditions, with their bodies becoming much more silvery in bright light. A broken band of black markings runs down the sides of the body, from the snout, passing through the eyes. Despite not being brightly colored, this is a subtly attractive fish.

Diet: Feeds on both prepared and live foods.

Natural habitat and behavior: Quite at home in rice paddies, they are often encountered in the fields themselves, where the depth of water may be no more than 2in (5cm). The water temperature here may rise to 99°F (37°C) during the heat of the day, so snakeskin gouramis then retreat to the larger drainage channels where the water remains cooler.

Aquarium conditions: A large tank, which is well planted and includes vegetation reaching to the surface, is ideal for snakeskin gouramis. In spite of their size, they are peaceful by nature, and can also prove to be rather shy, at least until they are established in their quarters. Although water conditions are not critical, the temperature should be within the range of 73–82°F (23–28°C), being increased toward the upper end to encourage spawning. As with other *Trichogaster* gouramis, females may produce over 1,000 eggs, although the bubblenest constructed by the male is relatively small in this species. The rearing needs of the fry are identical, with a plentiful supply of infusoria being needed at first. As always, keep the aquarium covered, to prevent the young gouramis from breathing cold air.

Colisa lalia

Distribution: Northeastern India and Bangladesh, present in the waterways of the Ganges, Bramaputra, and Jumuna.

Size: Up to 2.5in (6cm).

Form: The colorful males display alternating vertical orange and sky blue banding running down the sides of their bodies. The terminal rays on the dorsal fin of males taper to a point, rather than being rounded, as in females, which are of a silvery shade. Dwarf gouramis have been widely hybridized with other *Colisa* species, which has led to the development of a number of different varieties, they are generally infertile. These are often sold under names such as the sunset, thanks to its yellowish-orange coloration, and the neon, which is a brighter shade of blue, with its orange markings being broken up into irregular lines.

Diet: Prepared foods, including some vegetable matter.

Natural habitat and behavior: These gouramis form a strong pair bond, with male and female usually remaining in close proximity to each other. They are peaceful fish by nature, occurring in a range of habitats in the drainage areas of the major rivers where they occur.

Aquarium conditions: Dense planting is important, to provide adequate retreats for these gouramis (the most popular *Colisa* species), especially as they can be rather nervous. They are relatively undemanding about water conditions, providing these are not extreme, with a temperature between 72–82°F (22–28°C) suiting them well. Floating plants are also important, both as cover and for nest-building purposes, with male dwarf gouramis producing distinctive bubblenests incorporating leaves of vegetation such as crystalwort (*Riccia fluitans*). A male may mate with more than one female in succession, collecting the eggs in sequence and adding them to the nest. Within three days, the young fry are free-swimming and the adult gouramis must be removed by this stage, because they are otherwise likely to eat their offspring.

⭐ THICK-LIPPED GOURAMI

Colisa labiosa

Distribution: Occurs in the Irrawaddy river in Burma (Myanmar) and also present in Bangladesh.

Size: Typically between 2.3–4in (6–10cm).

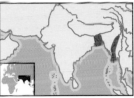

Form: Blue prominent on the underparts with banding on the sides of the body. Similar in appearance to the banded gourami (*C. fasciata*) but with a smaller head. Males also have red edging to their extended dorsal fin, with a rounded white edge to the anal fin. Females are easily discernible by their underlying duller, silvery-gray body shading.

Diet: Prepared foods and plant matter.

Natural habitat and behavior: These fish are found throughout most of the Irrawaddy, extending from northern areas right down to the port of Bassein. Their distinctive thick lips help them to browse on algae growing on submerged rocks. Although peaceful toward other aquarium occupants, males of this species can sometimes become extremely quarrelsome if housed in the company of others of their own kind, especially during the breeding period. Pairs should always be accommodated individually at this stage.

Aquarium conditions: A pH that is around neutral, with reasonably soft water conditions suits these fish well. A darkened base to the tank is preferred, and again, it should be well decorated with plants and bogwood, to provide cover. Males construct a large but fragile bubblenest, which is home to as many as 600 eggs laid by the female, and diligently transferred there by her partner. A stable water temperature, in spite of regular partial water changes, is vital for the subsequent development of the young. If infusoria cultures are not available as a rearing food initially, a special fry food for egg-laying fish can be offered. They can then be weaned gradually on to brine shrimp nauplii from the age of about 10 days onward. Cross-breeding with the banded gourami has resulted in fertile hybrids being produced, including a yellow variant.

Colisa chuna

Distribution: Northeastern India, in the Assam valley, extending to Bangladesh.

Size: Up to 2in (5cm).

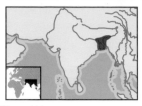

Form: One of the most beautiful members of what is a colorful genus, the honey gourami is so named because of its rich orange-red hue which extends over much of the male's body, aside from a diagonal area running from the eyes down to the anal fin, which is a dark shade of blue, bordering on black. Females are predominantly brownish, with the dark area seen in the male being a lighter shade of blue. There has been considerable disagreement over the correct scientific name for this species: it is also often referred to as *C. sota*.

Diet: Omnivorous, taking prepared foods, vegetable matter, and small live foods.

Natural habitat and behavior: It is not always as easy to sex this species as might be thought, because males that are under stress for any reason resemble females in coloration. These gouramis are highly territorial by nature, and so males especially should not be kept together, because otherwise the weaker individual is inevitably bullied. A breeding territory of 80sq. in (500sq cm) is vigorously defended by the resident male.

Aquarium conditions: As with other *Colisa* species, a tank for these gouramis should be well planted, and must include floating plants. The water temperature needs to be in the range of 72–82°F (22–28°C), and a slightly acidic to neutral pH is recommended, with a dGH reading of up to 15. The male constructs a bubblenest at the start of the breeding period, while the female's abdomen swells slightly as the eggs develop in her body. Hatching takes a day or so, with the young requiring infusoria as their first food, once they have absorbed their yolk sacs and are free-swimming. Examine honey gouramis carefully prior to purchase, as they have acquired something of a reputation for being susceptible to the *Oodinium* parasite, which is the cause of the condition known as velvet disease (see pages 105–106).

⭐ CHOCOLATE GOURAMI

Sphaerichthys osphronemoides

Distribution: Southeast Asia, occurring on the Malaysian peninsula, Sumatra, and Borneo.

Size: Up to 1.8in (5cm).

Form: Predominantly light chocolate-brown in color, with a series of light golden vertical bands around the body, with one just behind the eye, another encircling the middle of the body and another three on the abdomen, including the base of the caudal fin. A similar band runs horizontally from the strongly pointed snout to the eye, and a narrow line extends above the eyes. Males are discernible by the pointed rather than the rounded shape of their dorsal fin. There is also a red-finned form, recognized as a separate subspecies, *S. o. selatanensis*, originating from Borneo.

Diet: Live foods of various types—may also eat flake.

Natural habitat and behavior: Occurs in heavily vegetated, sluggish stretches of water. On Sumatra, these gouramis have been caught in water that has been likened to dark coffee in color.

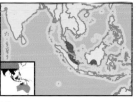

Aquarium conditions: This has proved a challenging species to keep, largely because of its water chemistry requirements. Chocolate gouramis require soft and acidic conditions, with readings of 2–3dGH and a pH around 6.0. Dense planting is also necessary, but the low mineral level in the water means that not all aquatic plants thrive in these surroundings. Certain cryptocornes, such as *C. walkeri*, can be recommended for this purpose however, as well as Indian water star (*Hygrophila polysperma*). The aquarium water should be filtered through peat, and the lighting should be subdued. Chocolate gouramis are peaceful, rather timid fish and do not thrive in the company of more robust companions. This has proved to be a maternal mouthbrooding species, with the female collecting the eggs after spawning, and retaining them in her mouth, with the fry emerging about two weeks later. They can then be reared on brine shrimp nauplii, growing to a length of 0.6in (1.5cm) within three weeks.

Trichopsis vittatus

Distribution: Southeast Asia, extending from Thailand to Vietnam and south to Sumatra and the Sunda islands.

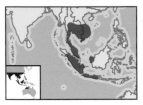

Size: Up to 2.8in (7cm).

Form: Varies in coloration through its wide range. Horizontal dark brownish stripes extend down the sides of the body, alternating with silvery bands, and a variable light blue suffusion, especially on the lower edge of the dorsal fin. A dark spot is often present behind the eyes. Sexing on appearance is extremely difficult, but the semi-transparent nature of the body does allow direct visualization of the female's reproductive tract in the form of a shadow running toward the tail, depending on the light. Mature males may also have longer, redder anal fins.

Diet: Omnivorous, taking flake and small live foods readily.

Natural habitat and behavior: Occurs in ponds and ditches, where the water is often dirty. Typically found in groups, congregating in schools below the leaves of aquatic plants, close to the surface. When spawning is imminent, the distinctive croaking calls of the males are heard, although females too are able to utter similar sounds.

Aquarium conditions: Acidic, soft water conditions are recommended for these gouramis, and some breeders keep them in aquariums with peat bases. The planting scheme is important, with floating plants being required as the male may build the nest under the cover of their leaves. Plants and other retreats in the main body of the water serve to provide cover for these gouramis, which are rather nervous by nature. Raising the water temperature up as high as 86°F (30°C) may help to trigger breeding activity, although this is not the easiest species to spawn successfully. Increasing the water softness may also help. The pair mate under the bubblenest itself, allowing the eggs to rise up. Relatively few eggs—often no more than 150—are laid at a single spawning. This species interbreed with the sparkling gourami (*T. schalleri*).

⬆ Croaking gourami
(*Trichopsis vittatus*)

➔ Croaking gourami
(*Trichopsis vittatus*
"trenggam kuantan")

⭐ DWARF CROAKING GOURAMI

Trichopsis pumilus

Distribution: Vietnam and Cambodia (Kampuchea), through Thailand and Malaysia to Sumatra.

Size: Up to 1.5in (4cm).

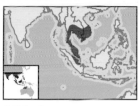

Form: The smaller size of this species is the best way to distinguish it from the croaking gourami (*T. vittatus*). Another point of distinction is that this species only has two broken horizontal lines running down each side of the body, rather than three as in the croaking gourami. Blue and red markings are present on the fins. The actual depth of their body coloration varies according to the level of illumination. Sexing is difficult, but males tend to have a more elongated, pointed anal fin. Again, examining the fish with a bright light behind the body helps to highlight the reproductive tract of the female.

Diet: Omnivorous, eating prepared diets such as flake and small live foods.

Natural habitat and behavior: Lives in shallow ditches and small ponds, where the water temperature can rise to as much as 91°F (33°C) during the day. Invariably encountered in small groups in heavily vegetated waters, where the oxygen level can be low.

Aquarium conditions: A well-planted aquarium incorporating floating plants is essential for these gouramis. Water conditions should be soft and slightly acidic, with the thermostat being set at 77–82°F (25–28°C). The eggs are laid in batches, with the female sometimes helping the male to transfer them to the bubblenest, which is not normally a particularly robust or conspicuous structure. It may be constructed either under floating plants, or sometimes even under rockwork in the aquarium. The croaking calls of the fish are most likely to be heard at this stage, and in spite of their small size, dwarf croaking gouramis can become quite aggressive in defense of their nest site when breeding. Hatching occurs after two days, with the young then becoming free-swimming after a similar interval. They require infusoria or a similar food at first.

FAMILY ANABANTIDAE

⭐ CLIMBING PERCH (WALKING PERCH)

Anabas testudineus

Distribution: Asia, being widely distributed in tropical areas from India to southern China and Indonesia.

Size: Up to 10in (25cm) but usually smaller.

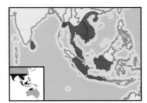

Form: Basically brownish, with silvery hues especially on the lower flanks, and odd darker markings on the body. Iris is orange. Males have a longer anal fin.

Diet: Eats a wide variety of foods, but prefer live food.

Natural habitat and behavior: Occurs in a variety of environments, including temporary pools, usually lurking in among vegetation, where the temperature can range from 59–86°F (15–30°C), depending both on the locality and time of year. May even be found in brackish water in some areas. Quite able to emerge on to land and breathe out of water, finding new pools as necessary. Usually moves after dark, when the risk of predation is lower. A yellow (xanthistic) form has been reported, but it is rarely seen, as is a second species, the high-bodied climbing perch (*A. oligolepis*).

Aquarium conditions: As might be expected, given the wide distribution of this species, climbing perches are relatively adaptable in their water chemistry requirements. They need a spacious aquarium, incorporating hardy plants that they are unlikely to damage. These anabantoids are shy by nature, but can also prove aggressive and predatory toward smaller fish. As a result, companions should be chosen carefully, but provided that their accommodation is sufficiently spacious, then they can be kept with larger *Trichogaster* gouramis or bushfish (*Ctenopoma* species). Their tank must be kept covered, and should be relatively shallow, especially for breeding purposes. There is no attempt at nest-building in this species, with the eggs simply being allowed to float to the surface after mating has occurred. The predatory instincts of the adult fish also mean the pair should be transferred elsewhere at this stage, with the eggs then hatching after approximately 24 hours. The fry should be reared initially on infusoria, and are mature at about 4in (12cm) in length. It is especially important that these fish are kept in a covered aquarium to prevent them possibly escaping at night.

⭐ SPOTTED CLIMBING PERCH (SPOTTED BUSH FISH; LEOPARD CTENOPOMA)

Ctenopoma acutirostre

Distribution: Western Africa, in the Congo basin, from Lisala to Kinshasa in Congo.

Size: Up to 6in (15cm).

Form: Relatively slim, flattened body shape, with relatively large eyes. The long dorsal fin reaches to the caudal fin, with a corresponding lengthy anal fin. The caudal fin itself is quite small and has a straight edge, with a prominent black spot at its base. Overall body color is yellowish-brown with darker spots. Males have body spines, sometimes described as "thorn fields," located behind the eyes and at the base of the caudal peduncle, which is short in this species.

Diet: Food tablets plus fresh or processed live foods.

Natural habitat and behavior: The prominent eyes of these fish suggest that they become more active toward dusk. Their deep mouth allows them literally to suck and swallow small creatures without

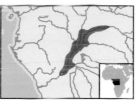

difficulty, and so they should not be housed with any fish significantly smaller in size. They are shy by nature and hide away, even becoming a more brownish shade overall on occasions, to blend in with their background.

Aquarium conditions: It is usually small individuals that are available, and they grow slowly, taking as long as three years to reach their adult size. They require soft water conditions, with a dGH reading of 2-4, and a pH close to neutral. The temperature itself should be in the range of 79-84°F (26-29°C). Lighting in the tank must be subdued, and there should be plenty of retreats provided, including bogwood. Relatively little has been documented about the breeding habits of the spotted climbing perch, but it is known to be a bubblenesting species, with the male being responsible for constructing the nest. Frequent feeds with rotifers are necessary for rearing the young fry at first, once they are free-swimming.

Ctenopoma kingsleyae

Distribution: West Africa, from the Gambia south to Zaire.

Size: Up to 5in (12cm) or more, but usually smaller.

Form: A plain-colored fish, with dark slate-gray upperparts and a lighter silvery sheen on the

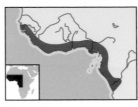

underparts. There is often a yellowish tinge on the anal and pectoral fins. Younger individuals have a distinctive blackish spot at the base of the caudal peduncle. In juvenile specimens of *C. kingsleyae* the tailspot is usually ringed in gold. Males can be identified by the presence of "thorn fields" of spikes in this area and also behind the eyes. The gill covers (opercula) are heavily serrated, compared with the closely related blunt-headed bushfish (*C. petherici*). As a result of the similarity between these species, it has been suggested that Kingsley's ctenopoma could simply be a color variant of the blunt-headed bushfish, which highlights the difficulty in classifying these particular anabantoids.

Natural habitat and behavior: Occurs both in flowing stretches of water, including forest streams, and also more open areas of water, in ditches. The natural coloration of these fish may be influenced by their environment, with those found in less-shaded localities being darker and displaying a more

pronounced greenish sheen on their bodies. Their appearance also changes with age.

Diet: Prepared foods and live foods.

Aquarium conditions: A large aquarium is needed for these bushfish, incorporating a darkened substrate, a well-planted interior and suitable retreats where the fish can hide. Water conditions are not especially vital, but a pH around neutral and a dGH up to 15 will suffice. Maintain the water temperature at 77–82°F (25–28°C). When spawning, a female can produce thousands of eggs which simply drift up and develop in the vegetation at the surface (hence the greater number of eggs produced initially). The adults show no parental care and since they are likely to eat their spawn, they cannot be left with their eggs. Hatching occurs after 24 hours or so, and then the young are free-swimming within a further 48 hours. The black marking at the base of the caudal fin starts to develop once they are one month old, with young fish of this species being more colorful than the adults. Do not mix Kingsley's ctenopomas with smaller companions as they grow, because they will prey on such fish, but they can be housed with any non-aggressive species of a similar size.

FAMILY OSPHRONEMIDAE

⭐ GIANT GOURAMI

Osphronemus goramy

Distribution: Widely distributed through southern Asia, from eastern India to China, south through the Malaysian peninsula to Java.

Size: Up to 28in (70cm).

Form: Protuberant mouth and pointed head. Although the coloration can differ widely, up to approximately 6in (15cm) in length, giant gouramis are grayish with darker transverse stripes on the body, and then start to acquire a distinctive reddish hue as they mature.

A golden color morph has also occurred, but the striped variety is now classified as a separate species, called the sevenstripe giant gourami (*O. septemfasciatus*). Male fish have longer, more pointed anal and dorsal fins.

Diet: Omnivorous, takes prepared foods. Older fish tend to be more vegetarian in their dietary preferences.

Natural habitat and behavior: The original natural range of these gouramis is unclear, because they are now widely farmed. Kept in large flooded areas, they

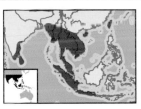

can reach 10in (25cm) by 12 months of age when maintained under favorable conditions. A fully grown giant gourami may weigh 15lb (7kg). Males construct a massive nest incorporating aquatic vegetation. This can measure 20in (50cm) in diameter, and may be up to 10in (25cm) high.

Aquarium conditions: This is not a species to be selected without careful thought as to the future. The size of these particular gouramis means that they require spacious surroundings, and they are liable to eat their tankmates as they outgrow them. Younger giant gouramis can prove territorial too, but they become more placid as they grow older. Their large appetites mean an aquarium for these gouramis must be well filtered. A slightly acidic pH reading is ideal, and they can tolerate quite hard water conditions, up to 25dGH. Although breeding in aquarium surroundings is unlikely, a successful spawning can give rise to over 20,000 eggs. The male watches over his offspring, and they grow rapidly, at a rate of up to 0.5in (1cm) each week for the first month.

FAMILY HELOSTOMATIDAE

⭐ KISSING GOURAMI

Helostoma temminckii

Distribution: Southeast Asia, occurring naturally in Thailand and Malaysia, plus islands including Sumatra and Borneo.

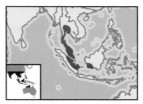

Size: Up to 12in (30cm), but usually only grows to 6in (15cm) or so.

Form: The natural color of these gouramis is silvery-gray, although the pink form has become popular in aquarium-keeping circles. There is also a less appealing mottled variant that has been bred. Sexing these gouramis even as adults is extremely difficult, although females may have broader backs when viewed from above.

Diet: Eats prepared foods and plant matter.

Natural habitat and behavior: Occurs in relatively large stretches of water, ranging from rivers and lakes to swamps. Their unique kissing behavior, when two individuals join lips, is not indicative of pair bonding—in fact it represents a trial of strength, with the weaker individual ultimately breaking off this contact.

Aquarium conditions: A large tank which is at least 40in (100cm) long is needed for these fish, and should contain relatively robust plants, which are less likely to be destroyed by these gouramis. They are useful in an aquarium for grazing algal growth, however, rarely touching vegetarian in their feeding habits than other species. Kissing gouramis prove reasonably adaptable in their water chemistry needs, and can kept within a temperature range of 72–86°F (22–30°C).

Breeding is uncommon in aquarium surroundings, and is much more likely to be achieved in a pond. The fish do not mature until they are approximately 5in (12cm) long. Females can produce over 10,000 eggs at a single spawning. The male kissing gourami makes little attempt if any to construct a bubblenest, and the eggs just float at the surface. An established culture of infusoria in the breeding setup is essential for rearing the fry, with the adult fish having to be removed once egg-laying has occurred.

FAMILY LUCIOCEPHALIDAE

⭐ PIKEHEAD

Luciocephalus pulcher

Distribution: Southeast Asia, ranging from the Malay peninsula to Sumatra, Borneo, and other islands.

Size: Up to 8in (20cm).

Form: Narrow, torpedolike body shape, with a prominent mouth and

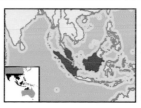

a powerful caudal fin. Predominantly brown in color, with two pale yellowish stripes running along the sides of the body, the upper one of which passes through the eye. This striped patterning becomes broken into spots in dominant males in breeding condition, while females become swollen with eggs. The anal fin is deeply divided, appearing to form two separate fins.

Diet: Feeds exclusively on live invertebrates and small fish.

Natural habitat and behavior: This is a highly predatory species, as reflected by its body shape. It inhabits stretches of still and gently flowing water, patrolling the middle areas in search of suitable prey. Food is sucked into the mouth, rather than being actively seized in the jaws. Pikeheads are sociable fish by nature, living in groups.

Aquarium conditions: This is not a species that is easy to maintain, thanks to its dietary requirements. Soft, slightly acidic water conditions are favored by these distinctive predators, with a temperature range of 72–84°F (22–29°C). The aquarium should be well planted, albeit with some open areas, and the lighting needs to be subdued. Pikeheads are ideally housed in a species-only setup, and must never be kept with smaller companions, which are likely to fall prey to them.

When displaying, the male uses his pelvic fins and inflates his throat, with the female subsequently laying as many as 90 eggs. These are collected up by the male, who broods them in his mouth for approximately 28 days. When the young finally emerge, they are already 0.5in (1.3cm) long. Mosquito larvae have been used successfully for rearing purposes, and also the fry of other labyrinth fish.

Further Reading

Alderton, David. *The International Encyclopedia of Tropical Freshwater Fish*. New York: Howell Book House, 1997.

Alderton, David.. *The Complete Guide to Fish Care*. London: Mitchell Beazley, 1998.

Alderton, David. *Starter Aquarium*. Irvine California: BowTie Press, 2002.

Andrews, Chris. *A Fishkeeper's Guide to Fish Breeding*. London: Salamander Books, 1986.

Andrews, Chris, Excell, A., and Carrington, N. *The Manual of Fish Health*. London: Salamander Books, 1988.

Axelrod, Herbert R., Burgess, Warren E., Pronek, N., and Walls, J.G. *Dr. Axelrod's Atlas of Freshwater Aquarium Fishes*. New Jersey: T.F.H. Publications, 1985.

Baensch, Hans A., and Riehl, Rudiger. *Aquarium Atlas* Vols 1–3. Melle: Baensch, 1987, 1993, 1996.

Banister, K., and Campbell, A. (Eds). *The Encyclopedia of Aquatic Life*. New York: Facts on File Inc., 1995, 1998, 2004.

Dawes, John. *Complete Encyclopedia of the Freshwater Aquarium*. Ontario: Firefly, 2001.

Goldstein, Robert J. *Bettas: A Complete Pet Owner's Manual*. New York: Barron's, 2001.

Hiscock, Peter. *Creating a Natural Aquarium*. Dorking: Interpet, 2000.

Jepson, Lance. *A Practical Guide to Keeping Healthy Fish in a Stable Environment*. Dorking: Interpet, 2001.

Lambert, Derek. *A Practical Guide to Breeding Your Freshwater Fish*. Dorking: Interpet, 2001.

Linke, Horst. *Labyrinth Fish—The Bubble-Nest Builders*. Plains: Tetra Press, 1991.

Pinter, Helmut. *Labyrinth Fish*. New York: Barron's, 1986.

Richter, Hans-Joachim. *Gouramis and other Anabantoids*. New Jersey: T.F.H. Publications, 1988.

Sandford, Gina. *The Questions and Answers Manual of the Tropical Freshwater Aquarium*. Abingdon: Andromeda Oxford, 1998.

Schafer, Frank. *All Labyrinths: Bettas Gouramis Snakeheads Nandids*. Morfelden-Walldorf: Verlag A.C.S., GmbH, 1997.

Scheurmann, Ines. *Aquarium Plants Manual*. New York: Barron's, 1993.

Vierke, Jörg. *Bettas, Gouramis and other Anabantoids: Labyrinth Fishes of the World*. New Jersey: T.F.H. Publications, 1988.

Web Sites

There are a number of groups with Web sites relating specifically to these fish. They include:

Anabantoid Society of Great Britain
http://aagb.org/

Communauté Internationale pour les Labyrinthidés (CIL):
http://cil.france.free.fr/index.html

International Betta Congress
http://ibcbettas.com/

Internationalen Gemeinschaft für Labyrinthfische (IGL) http://igl-home.de/

Nederlandse Vereniging voor Labyrintvissen
http://iglnl.netfirms.com/

A number of commercial Web sites also offer useful information and images, such as:

Bettas 'R Us http://www.bettasrus.com/
Top Bettas.com http://www.topbettas.com/

A useful general Web site is:

Fishlink Central http://www.fishlinkcentral.com/

Glossary

Acidic A reading on the pH scale below 7.0.

Adsorb The process whereby molecules passing through a filter can stick to a porous surface such as carbon.

Air sacs Structures connecting with the gut, which evolved in primitive fish to provide buoyancy.

Algae Microscopic plants present in water, which can coat glass, rockwork, and other surfaces in the aquarium, especially under conditions of high light intensity.

Alkaline A reading on the pH scale measuring above 7.0.

Ambush predator A predator that hunts by concealing its presence, so that it can ambush its target, rather than simply chasing it.

Anabantoids A collective term for fish that are classified as members of the suborder Anabantoidei. The families within this suborder are the Anabantidae, Belontiidae, Helostomatidae, Luciocephalidae, and Osphronemidae.

Anal fin Unpaired fin in front of the vent.

Biotope The fish and its natural environment.

Brackish Water conditions that are more saline than freshwater, but are not as salty as seawater itself. Typically encountered at the mouths of estuaries.

Bubblenest The structure made from air bubbles encased in mucus where the eggs of certain anabantoids are hatched.

Caudal fin The tailfin.

Caudal peduncle The area between the body and caudal fin.

Channoidei A suborder of fish that contains just one family, the Channidae, or snakeheads. These fish are considered to be closely related to the anabantoids.

Chemical filtration Typically describes the use of activated carbon to remove harmful substances from solution.

Chromosomes The strands on which the genes are located in the nucleus of cells.

Convergent evolution The way in which external environmental pressures have shaped the physical appearance of unrelated fish, so they appear similar.

Crown The center of a plant, from where new growth occurs.

Dechlorinator A product that removes harmful chlorine from local water supplies, making it safe for the fish.

Dorsal fin The prominent fin which lies farthest forward on the upper area of the back.

Dropsy Abnormal swelling of the body. May have infectious or noninfectious causes.

Estivate Means of surviving unfavorable environmental conditions by becoming inactive.

Family A group of fish that consists of members of different genera.

Fancy A strain of fish selectively bred for characteristic features such as coloration or fin shape.

Filter bed The medium, such as gravel, through which water passes as part of the filtration process.

Fins Projections on the fish's body that it uses for locomotion and display, as well as mating in some cases.

Flake Thin waferlike manufactured food for fish, which floats well on the water surface.

Free-swimming The stage at which young fish start to swim around their quarters for the first time.

Fry Young fish.

Genus/genera (pl) A group consisting of one or more species. (*See also*: monotypic genus).

GH Reflects the general or permanent hardness of a water sample; unaffected by boiling the water.

Gills The major means by which fish are able to extract oxygen from the water, located just behind the eyes on each side of the head.

Gondwanaland The prehistoric large southern continent that ultimately broke up to form much of today's earth surface.

Hard water Water that contains a relatively high level of dissolved calcium or magnesium salts.

Heaterstat Combined heater and thermostat unit for aquarium use.

Hybridization The successful mating of two different species together, which results in so-called hybrid offspring.

KH A measure of temporary hardness, resulting from bicarbonates or carbonates dissolved in the water, that can be reduced by boiling.

Ichthyologists Those who study fish.

Labyrinth fish Fish with labyrinth organs. Accepted as synonymous with anabantoids.

Labyrinth organs Auxiliary breathing organs located close to the gills that enable fish to breathe atmospheric air directly.

Lateral line A sensory system running down the sides of the fish's body, allowing it to sense vibrations in the water.

Length Measurement of fish is usually carried out in a straight line from the snout to the base of the caudal fin, which is itself excluded from the figure.

Mechanical filtration The direct removal of waste matter by filtration, which effectively sieves it out of the water.

Monotypic genus A genus comprised of a single species.

Mouthbrooder A fish that retains its fertilized eggs in its mouth until they hatch, and may also allow its young back there for a period afterward to escape danger.

Mulm The debris that can accumulate on the floor of the aquarium.

Nandidae A fish family that includes the badis or chameleon fish (*Badis badis*); fish in this family are considered by some authorities to be closely related to the anabantoids.

Nauplii The larval stage in the lifecycle of the brine shrimp *Artemia salina*, cultured as a rearing food for young fish.

New Tank Syndrome Describes the potential for sudden death of aquarium occupants resulting from a fatal buildup of ammonia and nitrite in a newly established tank where the filtration system is not working effectively.

Nitrogen cycle The breakdown of toxic ammonia produced by the fish into nitrite and less toxic nitrate, which is used by plants for healthy growth.

Omnivorous Eating both plant and animal matter.

Operculum The movable flap that covers the gills, and allows water to flow over them.

Pectoral fins The fins located on each side of the body behind the gills.

Pelvic fins The fins present in front of the anal fin.

pH The relative acidity or alkalinity of a solution, based on a logarithmic scale, so each unit change represents a tenfold alteration in concentration, with pH 7 being neutral. Low values reflect increasing acidity: higher figures indicate a progressively more alkaline solution.

Photosensitive Affected by light.

Photosynthesis Process by which plants manufacture their nutritional requirements using light and carbon dioxide.

Plankton Microscopic plant and animal life in the water.

Power filter A filtration unit that incorporates its own pump to drive water through the unit.

Quarantine The complete isolation of newly acquired fish for a period of time, to ensure they are healthy, before introducing them to others of their kind; or the removal of a sick fish to a separate tank to avoid cross-infections.

Rays Bony framework that provides the structural support for the fins.

Rotifer A minute aquatic invertebrate of the phylum Rotifera, common in freshwater plankton and a useful source of food, in particular for small fry.

Scales Protective covering present over the bodies of most fish.

Shoal Term used primarily in the UK to describe a group of fish, usually of the same species, which swim together; a school.

Soft water Water that is low in dissolved salts, as typified by rainwater.

Speciation The process of environmental selection pressures that lead to the creation of a species.

Species A group of fish that closely resemble each other and can interbreed.

Standards The specified criteria used by judges when assessing particular varieties of fish at shows.

Strain A line of fish specifically developed for particular characteristics such as color.

Substrate The floor covering in the aquarium or the base of the fish's natural habitat.

Swim bladder The fish's air-filled organ of buoyancy.

Taxonomy The science of identifying fish types and defining the relationships between them.

Teleosts A large group of fish, including anabantoids, which have supportive rays in their fins.

Tomite The free-swimming, infective stage of the microscopic parasite that causes white spot.

Undergravel filter A plate filter that fits right across the bottom of the aquarium.

Vascularization The presence of blood vessels in tissues.

Vent Ano-genital opening behind the anal fin.

Wallace's Line Discernible biological division in the distribution of species in Southeast Asia, arising from changes in sea level in the past. Named after Alfred Russel Wallace, who first identified this boundary in t he mid 19th century.

Yolk sac Source of nourishment for fry prior to and immediately after hatching.

Zoogeographic The way in which geographical features influence distribution of species.

Index